QUANTUM REVOLUTION II

QED: THE JEWEL OF PHYSICS

Vignettes in Physics
A series by G Venkataraman

A Hot Story
At the Speed of Light
Bhabha and His Magnificent Obsessions
Bose and His Statistics
Chandrasekhar and His Limit
Quantum Revolution (3 vols.)
1. The Breakthrough
2. QED: The Jewel of Physics
3. What is Reality?
Raman and His Effect
Saha and His Formula
The Many Phases of Matter
Why Are Things the Way They Are?
The Big and the Small (2 vols.)
1. Journey into the Microcosm—The Story of Elementary Particles
2. From the Microcosm to the Macrocosm—The Fascinating Link between Particle Physics and Cosmology

Vignettes in Physics

QUANTUM REVOLUTION II

QED: THE JEWEL OF PHYSICS

G. Venkataraman

Universities Press

QUANTUM REVOLUTION II – THE JEWEL OF PHYSICS

UNIVERSITIES PRESS (INDIA) PRIVATE LIMITED

Registered Office
3-6-747/1/A & 3-6-754/1, Himayatnagar
Hyderabad 500 029, Telangana, India
info@universitiespress.com; www.universitiespress.com

Distributed by
Orient Blackswan Private Limited

Registered Office
3-6-752 Himayatnagar, Hyderabad 500 029, Telangana, India

Other Offices
Bengaluru, Bhopal, Chennai, Guwahati, Hyderabad, Jaipur, Kolkata, Lucknow, Mumbai, New Delhi, Noida, Patna, Vijayawada

First Published 1994
Reprinted 1997, 2006, 2008, 2010, 2015, 2018

501488

ISBN: 978 81 7371 003 2

Printed at
Graphica Printers & Binders, Hyderabad 500 013

Published by
Universities Press (India) Private Limited
3-6-747/1/A & 3-6-754/1, Himayatnagar
Hyderabad 500 029, Telangana, India

Contents

Preface

To the adult reader

This book and others in this series written by me are inspired by the memory of my son Suresh who left this world soon after completing school. Suresh and I often used to discuss physics. It was then that I introduced him to the celebrated *Feynman Lectures*.

Hans Bethe has described Feynman as the most original scientist of this century. To that perhaps may be added the statement that Feynman was also the most scintillating teacher of physics in this century.

The Feynman Lectures are great but they are at the textbook level and meant for serious reading. Moreover, they are a bit expensive, at least for the average Indian student. It seemed to me that there was scope for small books on diverse topics in physics which would stimulate interest, making at least some of our young students take up later a serious study of physics and reach for the Feynman as well as the Landau classics.

Small books inevitably remind me of Gamow's famous volumes. They were wonderful, and stimulated me to no small extent. Times have changed, physics has grown and we clearly need other books, though written in the same spirit.

In attempting these volumes, I have chosen a style of my own. I have come across many books on popular science where elaborate sentences often tend to obscure the scientific essence. I have therefore opted for simple English, and I don't make any apologies for it. If a simple style was good enough for the great Enrico Fermi, it is also good enough for me. I have also employed at times a chatty style. This is deliberate. Feynman uses this with consummate skill, and I have decided to follow in his footsteps (whether I have succeeded or not, is for readers to say). This book is meant to be read for fun and excitement. It is a book you can even lie down in bed and read. Without going to sleep I hope!

Naturally I have some basic objectives, the most important of which is to stimulate the curiosity of the reader. Here and there the reader may fail to grasp some details, and in fact I have deliberately pitched things a bit high on occasions. But if the reader is able to experience at least in some small measure the *excitement* of science, then my purpose would have been achieved. Apart from excitement, I have also tried to convey that although we might draw boundaries and try to compartmentalise Nature into different subjects, she herself knows no such boundaries. So we can always start anywhere, take a random walk and catch a good glimpse of Nature's glory. Where she is concerned, all topics are 'fashionable'. There is today an unnecessary polarization of the young towards subjects that are supposed to be fashionable. To my mind this is unhealthy, and I have tried to counter it.

This series is essentially meant for the curious. With humility, I would like to regard it as some sort of a 'Junior Feynman Series', if one might call it that. With much love, and sadness, it is dedicated to the memory of Suresh who inspired it.

To the young reader

This is Part II of the trilogy on the Quantum Revolution, I hope you have read Part I in which I narrated the story of the birth of quantum mechanics; that background would be helpful. In Part I we came up to the early thirties when the triumphs of non-relativistic QM and the Dirac equation were followed by the "plague" or the crisis of the infinities. This book is all about that crisis and how it was contained. Notice I am using the word *contained* and not *solved*. You will find out the reason for this inside.

This volume would bring you up to the fifties. You will not only learn how the battle of infinities was fought, but more important, about a new approach to quantum mechanics as well. As usual there; was excitement attending the developments, and also a crop of heroes. I hope you would enjoy reading all about it.

Aknowledgements

Once again, Professors N. Mukunda and V. Balakrishnan came to my rescue and rendered valuable help by critically reviewing the draft manuscript and purging it of errors and inaccuracies. If any still survive, I am to be blamed! I also acknowledge with gratitude the help rendered by Mr. A. Ratnakar in collecting source material. The typescript was prepared as usual by Mrs. G. Naga Nirmala with her customary zeal and efficiency.

G. VENKATARAMAN

1 *The Prelude*

> The theory was troubled. If you calculated something roughly, it would give a reasonable answer. But if you tried to compute it more accurately, you would find that the correction you thought was going to be small was in fact very large—in fact, it was *infinity*! So it turned out you couldn't really compute *anything* beyond a certain accuracy.
>
> *Feynman*

1.1 Introduction

Modern Quantum Electro Dynamics (QED) is the creation of three theoretical physicists Sin-Itiro Tomonaga of Japan, Julian Schwinger of America and Richard Feynman, also of America. They made their discoveries independently. About this theory, the noted physicist Freeman Dyson says:

> This is the theory which brought order and harmony into the vast middle ground of physics, excluding gravitation on the one side and nuclear forces on the other, but including the laws of atomic structure, radiation, creation and annihilation of particles, solid-state physics, plasma physics, maser and laser technology, optical and microwave spectroscopy, electronics and chemistry. Quantum electrodynamics unifies all these diverse phenomena into a small number of principles of great generality and elegance, weaving together special relativity and quantum mechanics in a seamless fabric. It is in a certain sense the most perfect and the most highly developed part of physics.

Feynman refers to it as "the jewel of physics—our proudest possession." In this chapter I shall briefly trace the events leading to the "plague of infinities" referred to in the preface.

My survey will be brief since many of the details are available in Part I. QED emerged as the result of a synthesis of activities on two fronts—studies on atomic structure and studies on the quantum aspects of radiation. Let us start with atomic structure.

Till the discovery of the electron in 1897, the atom was considered to be a sphere and the *ultimate* building block of matter, meaning that it was indivisible. And when in 1910 Rutherford discovered the (atomic) nucleus, it was not only clear that the atom *was* divisible, but also that it had an internal structure of its own. To be ascertained now was the precise nature of this internal structure. The planetary model of the atom was a strong candidate but classical mechanics which worked in the case of the Solar system failed to oblige in the case of the atom. In 1913, Bohr "suspended" both classical mechanics and classical electrodynamics, offering instead his celebrated atom model. No doubt Bohr swept many things under the rug but then nothing succeeds like success; and the Bohr model was a runaway success, for a while that is. But soon all kinds of problems cropped up and everyone hungered for a systematic set of rules which would lead to correct results for any set of particles, displaying the required features like the quantisation of energy, the quantisation of angular momentum, etc.

The much-longed for mechanics finally came into being in the mid-twenties, thanks mainly to Heisenberg, Schroedinger and Dirac, with of course important supporting contributions from Born, Jordan, Kramers and Pauli and others. And so by late 1926 there was a quantum theory of matter. No doubt this theory gave a good account of things like the energy levels of atoms and so forth but that was not enough. You would recall from Part I that the discovery of quantum mechanics was spurred by attempts to calculate the intensity of spectral lines. With a new mechanics now available, there was fresh incentive to tackle the problem of line intensity.

A spectral line is emitted when an atom makes a transition from one energy level to a lower one. The transition occurs when the atom is disturbed. Disturbed by what? Maybe by an external force (or electromagnetic field). Given an external perturbing agency, Schroedinger showed how the effects of the perturbation—in this case a transition to a lower atomic level—could be calculated. According to this picture, an atom cannot spontaneously emit radiation. But this was contrary to experience. And though Einstein had introduced the concept of spontaneous emission as early as 1917, there was, even as late as 1926, no theory available for demonstrating the existence of spontaneous emission and the various effects connected with it.

1.2 QED I

In 1927, Dirac gave a theory which, among other things, made possible such a calculation. Dirac's paper was entitled *The Quantum Theory of the Emission and Absorption of Radiation,* and in the opening para he says:

> The new quantum theory [meaning that of Heisenberg and Schroedinger] based on the assumption that the dynamical variables do not obey the commutative law of multiplication, has by now been developed sufficiently to form a complete theory of dynamics. One can treat mathematically the problem of any dynamical system composed of a number of particles with instantaneous forces acting between them, provided it is describable by a Hamiltonian function, and one can interpret the mathematics physically by quite a definite general method. On the other hand, hardly anything has been done up to the present on quantum electrodynamics.

This 1927-theory of Dirac may be regarded as QED, version I. It is based on a simple idea. Instead of considering an atom and the radiation field with which it interacts as two distinct systems, Dirac treated them as a single system whose Hamiltonian is made up of three parts: H_A representing the energy of the atom, H_R representing the energy of the radiation field and H_I representing the coupling energy of the atom and the radiation field.

Dirac treated radiation as a quantum field. Before considering a quantum field, let us first consider a classical field. Dyson describes the latter as follows:

> A classical field is a kind of tension or stress which can exist in empty space in the absence of matter. It reveals itself by producing forces, which act on any material objects that happen to lie in the space the field occupies.

The standard example of a classical field is the electromagnetic field. The state of the field is described by giving the strength of the electric and magnetic fields at all points of space. As Dyson puts it:

> This is the characteristic mathematical property of a classical field: it is an undefined something which can exist throughout a volume of space and which is described by sets of numbers, each set denoting the field strength and direction at a single point in the space.

Consider now the electric and the magnetic fields E and H associated with radiation of frequency v, say (angular frequency $\omega = 2\pi v$). The electromagnetic energy W contained in a volume Ω is given by

$$W = \Omega\left(\overline{E}^2 + \overline{H}^2\right)/8\pi. \tag{1.1}$$

Here $\overline{E}^2$ and $\overline{H}^2$ describe suitable average values. We now introduce suitable variables q and p in place of E and H and make use of Maxwell's equation. After a bit of algebra, one can show that (1.1) can be rewritten as

$$W = (1/2)\left(p^2 + \omega^2 q^2\right) \tag{1.2}$$

which has the form of the Hamiltonian of a one-dimensional oscillator. Since all frequencies are present in the radiation contained in the cavity, the radiation Hamiltonian must be written as a sum over the contributions of the various frequencies, namely,

$$H_R = (1/2)\sum_s \left(p_s^2 + \omega_s^2 q_s^2\right). \tag{1.3}$$

Following the development of quantum mechanics, Born, Heisenberg and Jordan showed how the new mechanics could be applied to the radiation field. Essentially one made the p's and the q's obey proper commutation relations. The outcome:

1. Associated with oscillator of frequency v_s, there is a spectrum of energy levels

   $$\varepsilon(n_s) = (n_s + 1/2)hv_s \quad n_s = 0, 1, 2, \ldots$$

2. An oscillator excited to level with quantum number n_s is equivalent to the presence of n_s photons of frequency v_s.
3. Increase of n_s corresponds to the emission (or creation) of photons while decrease corresponds to photon absorption (or annihilation). The state of the radiation field can thus be specified by writing down in an ordered sequence the numbers of photons present corresponding to the various frequencies. This is the *occupation number representation*.
4. Even if all the occupation numbers are zero, the field has a *zero-point energy* given by $\sum_s (1/2)hv_s$.

In his trend-setting paper of 1927, Dirac essentially adopted the above picture for the (quantum) radiation field.

As I said earlier, we have H_A the Hamiltonian for the atom and H_R the Hamiltonian for the radiation field. Together $H_0 = H_A + H_R$ represents the Hamiltonian of the combined but uncoupled system. This means that the atom and the radiation mind their own business and do not interact with each other. In practice we know that they do interact because the current associated with the electron in the atom produces a radiation field which can react or back couple with the atom. So one must allow for an interaction Hamiltonian say, H_I, which produces this back coupling.

Notation: Using the Dirac *ket* notation, we write the state of the combined system (i.e., atom plus radiation) as $|i; n_1, n_2, ..., n_s, ...\rangle$. Suppose that due to H_I the atom makes a transition from level i to level $(i - 1)$. Let $E_i - E_{(i-1)} = h\nu_s$. This implies that during the downward transition mentioned above, one photon of frequency ν_s would be emitted causing n_s to change to $n_s + 1$. Thus the combined system undergoes the following change:

Initial state	Final state
$\|i; n_1, ..., n_s, ...\rangle$	$\|i-1; n_1, ..., (n_s+1), ...\rangle$

Dirac's paper gives the rules for calculating the rate at which this transition would occur etc. All that is a matter of detail and I shall not consider it here.

What is this theory good for? In a brilliant series of lectures delivered in America in 1932, Enrico Fermi explained that to an eager audience; a sample of what he dealt with can be found in Box 1.1. Here I would like to call attention to a couple of important points. To start with? Dirac's theory allowed for the first time the back reaction or back coupling to be handled (as described in Box 1.1).

Box 1.1 This is a capsule summary of Fermi's lecture notes which appeared as an article in the *Reviews of Modern Physics* and which later became a bible to many an aspiring student. Fermi first writes down a three-part Hamiltonian $H = H_A + H_R + H_I$ like that introduced in the text. Starting from this, he discusses emission from an excited atom, Compton effect, Doppler effect and so on. In every case, H_I is treated as a perturbation and results are obtained to the lowest order in perturbation theory. The essence of his approach can be understood by considering the case of emission of radiation by an atom in an excited state say, m. Suppose the radiation is emitted by the atom going to the state n; let ν_{nm} be the frequency of the emitted radiation. In principle, the atom can emit lines of different frequencies. Call them ν_1, ν_2, ... Obviously, ν_{nm} belongs to this set of allowed frequencies.

We now turn our attention to the radiation field. We describe its status by specifying the numbers of photons of various frequencies, i.e., the numbers n_1, n_2, ... Suppose that initially all these numbers are zero. We can, using the Dirac notation, write the state of the combined system (atom + radiation field) as

$$|m; 0. 0, \ldots\rangle$$

This is the status before the line ν_{nm} is emitted. After the emission is completed, the state is changed to

$$|n; 0, 0, \ldots, 0, 1, 0, \ldots\rangle$$

where unity is entered against n_{nm}.

We now consider thc amplitudes of these two states which, for simplicity, we write as a_{I} and a_{II} respectively. Obviously, these two amplitudes would depend on time and at the beginning of the emission process we would have $a_{\text{I}}(t = 0) = 1$ and $a_{\text{II}}(t = 0) = 0$. At the end of the process, i.e., at $t = \infty$, we would have $a_{\text{I}}(t = \infty) = 0$ and $a_{\text{II}}(t = \infty) = 1$. A complete description of emission is obtained when one has the complete histories of a_{I} and a_{II}. This Fermi obtains by solving appropriate equations of motion. It leads him eventually (i) to the lifetime of state m and (ii) the width of the spectral line (this is related to the lifetime).

In the Bohr model of the atom, there is *NO* mechanism to trigger the transition $m \rightarrow n$. One simply says the atom jumps. In ordinary QM, the atom can go from level m to level n, provided there is an *external* perturbation. Dirac's QED (version I) allowed one (as Fermi showed) to calculate the *spontaneous* decay of an excited state. This decay occurs because of back coupling mentioned in the text. Operationally, the back coupling is triggered by H_I.

The second point is a bit technical. The perturbing part of the Hamiltonian, i.e., H_I, has two parts namely $\hat{\text{p}} \cdot \hat{\text{A}}$ and $\hat{\text{A}}^2$. Here $\hat{\text{p}}$ is the momentum operator for the electron and $\hat{\text{A}}$ is what is called the vector potential of the electromagnetic field. For a moment, let us not worry about what exactly Â is. The difference between the two perturbation terms is that in one of them Â acts only once whereas in the other Â acts twice. The version of QED developed after the advent of the Dirac equation, i.e., QED II, does not have the analogue of the $\hat{A}^2$ type of perturbation; it has only the counterpart of $\hat{p} \cdot \hat{A}$.

1.3 Dirac's theory of the electron

We now come to the celebrated Dirac theory of the electron, a major turning point. Its virtue was that it paid due respect to the special theory of relativity, ignored by the earlier versions of QM due to Heisenberg and Schroedinger. This is what Dyson refers to as the *seamless weaving together of QM and special relativity*. As you know from Part I, thanks to the Dirac equation, the electron spin received a natural description. It also, brought in the negative-energy states about which now a few comments.

In the beginning these negative-energy states were rather unwelcome but they have remained with us, completely changing the character of physics. Skipping the history (for which see Part I), I would like to mention the following:

1. The negative-energy states are normally filled with electrons, with due regard to the Pauli exclusion principle.
2. Transitions are possible between the positive and the negative- energy states.
3. When a negative-energy electron makes a transition to a positive-energy state, *a hole* is produced is the negative-energy states. This hole behaves like an electron with a positive charge and is called *positron*.

1.4 Going back in time

Feynman introduced the radical idea, that holes in negative-energy state represent the states of electrons *moving backwards in time*. Since we shall be using this idea extensively later, a few words of explanation are necessary.

Figure 1.1 (a) shows a possible world line for an electron moving in one dimension. (Space-time diagrams and world lines are explained in the companion volume *At the Speed of Light*.) The electron leaves the space point x_1 at time t_1 and eventually arrives at the space point x_2 at time t_2. In between it meanders, and the world line portrays

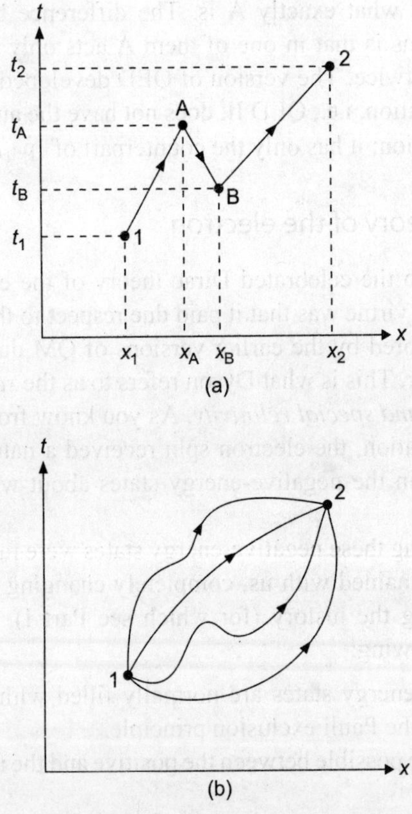

Fig. 1.1 (a) World line for an electron. Observe that between A and B, the electron goes back in time. As explained in text, one can also view this as a positron going (forward in time) from B to A. (b) illustrates the many paths for going from 1 to 2. Feynman discovered that QM could be reformulated in terms of these paths. This is the path-integral method which is discussed further in Chapter 4.

this meandering. In the space dimension, the electron never moves backwards, i.e., it always goes forward: $x_1 \rightarrow x_A \rightarrow x_B \rightarrow x_2$. But in the time dimension, something interesting happens. At the instant t_A, the electron decides to go backwards! It keeps doing so till time t_B when it decides to go forward in time once again. Thus the scenario may be described as follows:

1 → A: Electron moves forward in space. Electron also moves forward in time.

A → B: Electron continues to move forward in space, but moves backwards in time.

B → 2: Electron once again moves forward both in space and in time.

The above is Feynman's way of looking at things. The traditional view point is completely different. According to it:

- At t_1, only the electron is present.
- At t_B, somewhere else in space (i.e., at x_B), an electron – hole pair is created.
- Between t_B and t_A, the electron (e^-) and the hole or the positron (e^+) go off in different directions, the positron towards x_1 and the electron towards x_2. At t_A the electron which was originally at x_1 and the positron created at x_B meet and annihilate.
- Between t_A and t_2, only one electron is present.
- The position is never seen ; it has only a virtual existence.

In both cases, the electron starts at (x_1, t_1) and ends at (x_2, t_2). The world line has not changed; only a new interpretation has been given to it by Feynman. Such an interpretation is both convenient and fruitful because in quantum mechanics, the *total* amplitude for an electron to go from (x_1, t_1) to (x_2, t_2) is the sum of the amplitudes for each of the possible paths linking the space-time points—see Fig. 1.1(b). With Feynman's way of looking at things, we don't have to worry about where and when positrons appear and where and when they disappear.

In a nutshell, if one thinks of electrons and positrons, then one has to have distinct world lines for the electron and the positron. However, if one considers only the electron, then there is only one world line to worry about. It is all a matter of one's viewpoint, and Feynman brings this home with a beautiful analogy. He says:

> It is as though a bombardier flying low over a road suddenly sees three roads and it is only when two of them come together and disappear again that he realises that he has simply passed over a long switchback in a single road.
>
> This over-all space-time view leads to considerable simplification in many problems.

More about all this later on.

1.5 QED II

Let us get back to the Dirac equation. Dirac proposed it for describing a single electron, with due regard to the requirements of special relativity. Then came the unpleasant negative energy states, which, after some hesitation, were populated. As a result, the one-electron theory suddenly became a many-electron theory. Also, there was now the possibility of creating and annihilating particles. Further, since electron annihilation produces radiation, there was no longer any question of having a theory of electrons alone. In other words, *an integrated package with radiation properly built-in was necessary to make Dirac's theory complete*. For this, two things had to be done. First the particles had to be described in terms of fields. Second, the field had to be quantised. I have briefly touched upon these aspects in Part I but a gist of that is worth repeating.

In classical physics, a collection of particles can be represented by a suitable field $\psi(\mathrm{r}, t)$. One does this, for example, in fluid mechanics. One does a somewhat similar thing when one deals with many (identical) particles in non-relativistic quantum mechanics, i.e., one introduces a quantum field $\psi(\mathrm{r}, t)$. The field amplitude ψ would satisfy a Schroedinger equation. However, notwithstanding the appearance of the Planck's constant h in the Schroedinger equation, the particle field is not yet a quantum entity. To make it so, the field amplitude ψ has to be treated as an operator which is done via suitable anti-commutation relations. This process which is called *second quantisation* applies equally well to the field of Dirac particles. See also Box 1.2.

Box 1.2 QED is an example of a quantum field theory. I have already mentioned something about fields in Part I, and have quoted Dyson here. The moment we talk of a field, we must be able to specify its amplitude as a function of space (r) and time (t). The amplitude could refer to a scalar field, a vector field or a spinor field. In the case of the electromagnetic field, we deal with a vector field amplitude $\mathrm{A}(\mathrm{r}, t)$ and in the case of the Dirac electron, we deal with a spinor field $\psi(\mathrm{r}, t)$.

Fields are needed for describing particles—A for describing photons and ψ for describing electrons. Field theory is most useful when one deals with many particles, as in QED. Having a field amplitude like ψ, for example, does not mean one is ready for dealing with a many-particle system. ψ, you will recall, comes from the Dirac equation which is for *one* electron. To prepare it for use in a many-electron environment, one must first declare ψ as an operator and next specify the anti-commutator {ψ (r, t), ψ (r′, t)}. For A, we would have to write down the commutator. This step is called *second quantisation*.

At the practical working level, one creates or annihilates photons in a particular state k, say. For this purpose, one defines operators $a_k^\dagger$ and a_k in terms of A. Likewise, in the case of electrons, one defines creation and annihilation operators , $b_k^\dagger$, b_k in terms of ψ. In this volume we will not encounter these operators because we would mostly be following Feynman's approach to QED.

Next we consider the electromagnetic field. In classical physics, a comprehensive description of it is provided by Maxwell's equations. In our earlier discussions on radiation, we conveniently ignored the *source of radiation* which always consists of moving charges. Besides, a good theory must be sufficiently general but unfortunately, a general electromagnetic field cannot be built up simply by superposing transverse electromagnetic waves alone (which is what we did earlier). So the earlier discussion has to be extended so as to cover the quantisation of a general electromagnetic field. This is a bit of a technical affair, and for those interested a glimpse of the issues involved is given in the Appendix to this chapter.

In 1933, Dirac set the ball rolling as far as the quantisation of the Dirac field was concerned. In turn, this led to the "integrated package" referred to above. After seeing one of Dirac's papers on the subject, Pauli wrote a letter to Heisenberg which he signed, "Yours, drowned in Dirac's formulae, W. Pauli." Replying to it Heisenberg said, "I regard Dirac's theory as learned trash … which no one can take seriously." But all this scepticism was to change. Dirac's hole theory as it was caHed, was the only theory available and eventually everyone came back to it.

It is interesting to recall one touch added to it. Because Dirac's theory is completely symmetric in regard to electrons and positrons, Heisenberg postulated two fields: an electron or matter field, and a positron or anti-matter field. These two fields were allowed to interact with the quantised electromagnetic field. The main virtue of introducing this "symmetry" was that both the electrons and the positron equations contributed their own respective seas of filied negative energy states. But since these seas were of opposite charge, they cancelled each other. This simplified some problems. I shall refer to the relativistic version of QED based on the Dirac equation as QED II, calling the 1927 non-relativistic treatment of Dirac as QED I.

1.6 Infinities in classical electrodynamics

Not everything was well with the "new, improved" version of QED, i.e., QED II. There were all sorts of troubles and Heisenberg was prompted to remark: "I had the impression that in quantum theory [i.e., the theory of Heisenberg and Schroedinger] we had come back to the harbour, into the port. Dirac's paper threw us out into the sea again." Which brings us to the plague of infinities.

Electrodynamics is a formalism for calculating various quantities arising out of the interaction between charges and fields. When I referred to infinity above, I meant an infinite answer for a quantity which one knows to be finite. If one gets infinity as the answer in place of the correct finite one, then clearly something is wrong somewhere. QED II was giving infinite answers in a number of cases and everyone was Stuck until a fix was finally found in the late forties. QED with this fix would be referred to as QED III. Interestingly, infinities were known even in classical electrodynamics and so let us start with them.

According to electrostatics, an electron at rest is surrounded by an electrostatic field whose value at distance r is given by

$$\varepsilon(r)=\left(e^2/r\right). \tag{1.4}$$

If we consider a cell of unit volume at distance r, the energy content of the cell is $(1/8\pi)\varepsilon^2(r)$. The total electrostatic energy E is therefore obtained by integrating this energy over whole of space, i.e.,

$$E=\frac{1}{8\pi}\int\varepsilon^2(r)\,dv. \tag{1.5}$$

The question now arises about the range of integration. Obviously the upper limit would be infinity. What about the lower limit? This of course depends on the size of the electron. Normally we think of the electron as a point charge but can we be sure? Lorentz who was the first to develop a theory of the electron worried about this question. He assumed that the electron was a sphere of radius a. When this assumption is used in (1.5), one obtains

$$E=\frac{e^2}{2a}. \tag{1.6}$$

At this stage, let me quote Feynman.

> It is all fine until we set *a* equal to zero for a point charge [whereupon we get $E = \infty$]—there's the great difficulty... What's wrong with an infinite energy? If the energy can't get out, but must stay there forever, is there any real difficulty with an infinite energy? Of course, a quantity that comes out as infinite may be annoying, but what really matters is only whether there are any *observable* physical effects. To answer this question, we must turn to something else besides the energy.
>
> Suppose we ask how the energy *changes* when we *move* the charge. Then, if the *changes* are infinite, we will be in trouble.

Indeed one is. When the electron is moved with a uniform velocity v say, ($v \ll c$), the electric field generated by the electron motion acquires a momentum. Writing this momentum as $m_{em}.v$, we find that the electromagnetic field acts as if the electron had *a mass purely electromagnetic in origin*. Calculations show that this mass mem is given by

$$m_{em} = \frac{2}{3}\frac{e^2}{ac^2}. \tag{1.7}$$

This raises an interesting question: What is mass? In mechanics, we always assume that a particle has a mass. Where does this mass come from? Electrodynamics suggests that mass is just the effect of charged particles moving. Of course this does not rule out other possible sources of origin for the mass. So let us say there are two kinds of mass associated with the electron—one, "mechanical" which we denote as m_0 and the other which is electromagnetic in origin which we write as m_{em}. What we observe is the total mass ($m_0 + m_{em}$)—see also Box 1.3.

> **Box 1.3** It is interesting to compare the neutron with the proton. They are practically alike, except for the fact that the neutron is electrically neutral while the proton carries an electric charge. If the neutron mass is all "mechanical", then the proton should have m extra mass that is electromagnetic in origin. In other words, the observed masses of the neutron and the proton should be different. Indeed this is so but the trouble is that the neutron is heavier!

Before we start looking for trouble (!) suppose for a moment $m_0 = 0$, i.e., the mass of the electron is purely electromagnetic. We then find

$$a = \frac{2}{3}\frac{e^2}{m_{em}c^2}. \tag{1.8}$$

Since the mass is assumed to be entirely electromagnetic in origin, we might as well write the observed mass m_{exp} (= 9.1×10^{-28} gm) in place of m_{em} in (1.8). We would think that $a = (2/3)(e^2/m_{exp}c^2)$ would define the electron radius. Instead, the quantity $r_0 = (e^2/m_{exp}\,c^2) \sim 2.82 \times 10^{-13}$ cm is traditionally taken as the "classical electron radius". The 2/3 factor occurring in the definition of a depends on how the electric charge is actually distributed in the sphere of radius a. Different models of charge distributions can give different numerical factors and so, to make life easy, one defines r_0 as the "nominal" radius—notice that it is free from numerical factors.

Now for the trouble. If the electron is indeed a charged sphere, what is there to prevent this sphere from exploding on account of repulsion between its parts? Such an explosion would not occur if the radius a is zero but then the mass becomes infinity. In other words, finite radius for the electron produces one kind of difficulty, namely instability, while zero radius produces another, namely the mass becomes infinite. Problem! By the way, associated with mass one can define an energy via the Einstein equation $E = mc^2$. This energy is called the *self-energy*. When mass diverges, so does the self-energy.

This self-energy crisis is not merely a problem but a big disappointment as well, because, as Feynman puts it, Maxwell's celebrated theory "which is such a beautiful success in explaining so many phenomena, ultimately falls on its face". These difficulties are associated with the basic concepts of classical electromagnetism, and are not solved by quantum theory. In fact, quantum theory brings its own quota of trouble which I shall shortly mention. In Chapter 4, I shall return to some of these issues.

Let us continue with classical electromagnetic theory. The advent of special relativity made the problem even more acute. According to relativity, a body of finite extension cannot be rigid. If the electron had a finite radius, then it would be like putty when travelling at high speeds, which one cannot admit. So it must have zero radius, i.e., it must be a point particle in which case the self-energy becomes infinite.

1.7 Infinities in QED II

We come now to non-relativistic quantum mechanics. The Schroedinger equation for the hydrogen atom describes the electron without any reference to its size. Implicitly, the electron is treated as if it were a point particle. Once again the question arises about the self-energy, this time in quantum mechanics. Heisenberg and Pauli studied it with reference to QED I and found that the self-energy tends to infinity as the electron radius $a \to 0$. Trouble again.

After this came the Dirac equation and QED II, and with it a whole new bunch of infinities appeared! Basically they were of three types; an infinity due to infinite charge of the vacuum, an infinite mass due to self-energy effects and an infinity due to vacuum polarisation.

At this point we must be careful to note that there are actually two types of vacuum one has to deal with namely, that associated with the electron field and that associated with the electromagnetic field. Normally, we are used to thinking of the vacuum as a state of emptiness. In quantum field theory, this is not so. For example, the vacuum state of the electromagnetic field corresponds to all the radiation oscillators being in their quiescent state. Nevertheless, thanks to zero-point oscillations, there is infinite energy in the vacuum.

Turning to the vacuum of the electron field, in the Dirac theory, the negative-energy states are filled, leading to the so-called Dirac sea. Thus the vacuum now acquired infinite charge which was an embarassment. Heisenberg contained the problem by introducing two Dirac seas as I explained earlier. Today everyone accepts the idea of the Dirac sea without a murmur but in those days, the idea of negative-energy states was not exactly popular. In fact, Pauli and Weisskopf developed a relativistic theory for spin zero particles which was free from such states. Pauli was proud of this theory and referred to their paper as the anti-Dirac paper!

Pauli's prejudices notwithstanding, people realised that for the electron one *had* to use the Dirac equation, and therefore QED also *had* to be based on that equation; there was no getting away from that. And then in the early thirties, the roof gave way!

To explain this, I must make a reference to what happens in perturbation theory. Perturbation calculations are made to various orders, first-order, second order, etc., the order being determined by how many times the peiturbation acts. In using a perturbation approach, it is assumed that the perturbation is weak. To get a feel for the whole process, let us consider some numbers.

Suppose a quantity A is computed using perturbation theory. Let 1.342, say be the value obtained for A in the first-order. If the value obtained in second-order is 1,657, then the second-order correction is $1.657 - 1.342 = 0.315$. Notice that 0.315 is less than 1.342. The third-order correction would be less than 0.315, the fourth-order correction would be less than that of the third-order and so on. Therefore, when perturbation theory is legitimately used, the corrections get smaller and smaller and the accuracy of the answer is progressively improved as one goes to higher and higher orders.

In QED, the interaction between the particles and the electromagnetic fields is regarded as a perturbation. When QED II was used for making calculations, it gave reasonable answers in the lowest order. Encouraged, people then went to higher orders with the hope of improving the accuracy of their answers, when lo and behold, they encountered infinities! See the quotation from Feynman at the beginning of this chapter.

The case of the electron self-energy provides a classic example. In 1934, Weisskopf used the Dirac theory and obtained the following result:

$$\text{S.E} = c^2\left\{m_0.\pi\left(e^2/hc\right)\log\left(\lambda_c/a\right)\right\}. \tag{1.9}$$

Here $\lambda_c = (h/m_0c)$ is the Compton wavelength of the electron. (See also Box 1.4).

Box 1.4 Actually, Weisskopf made a trivial mistake apid got the result that the self-energy diverged as a power law, i.e., like x^n. Furry in America reading Weisskopf's paper realised that an error had been committed and wrote to Weisskopf that the correct answer was ~ log x, which made the infinity a lot weaker. Thereupon, Weisskopf published an erratum, i.e., a small note correcting his mistake. Recalling that event, Weisskopf later said:

> It shows the courtesy of physicists that time, that Furry didn't publish ... But that wouldn't happen today. Today the corresponding Furry would publish a paper and say that I was wrong. So this is why on every possible occasion I say how grateful I am to Furry. Because some of my fame comes from this—it is always connected with my name—and actually it was Furry.

The self-energy diverges as log(l/a) as $a \to 0$. This is the famous logarithmic divergence. True this is better than the (1/a) divergence of classical physics—see (1.6)—but it is bad news nevertheless.

Since S.E diverges, so does the mass, which is not acceptable since we know the mass of the electron is finite. In fact it is ~ 9.1×10^{-28}gm.

Now the self-energy implies an electromagnetic mass mem. As a result, one could argue as follows: Take m_0 in (1.9) to be the mechanical mass m_0. Now let a decrease. When a shrinks to 10^{-72} cm, m_{em} is barely 6 times larger than m_0 which is not much of an increase. In fact, by the time a comes down to 10^{-55} cm, the effects of general relativity start becoming important; and they have been ignored here. So it might be suggested that the divergence of (1.9) need not be taken too seriously. True, general relativity might come to the rescue, but the point is that QED II as it stands, does give an infinite answer.

Having considered the infinite charge and the infinite mass, we now turn to vacuum polarisation. This is a subtle effect and a truly quantum phenomenon. You will recall that prior to relativity, the vacuum was supposed to be filled with a mysterious substance called the ether, absolutely vital for ensuring the propagation of light. The famous Michelson-Morley experiment and the theory of relativity together dealt a blow to the ether (see the companion volume *At the Speed of Light*) and the vacuum became empty once again. But with the advent of the Dirac theory it became filled once more, this time in a different sort of way. Thanks to the Dirac sea, there was no more any such thing as an isolated electron; there was always the "full" vacuum in the background.

Now even though the vacuum, i.e., the Dirac sea is notionally full, once in a while an electron in a negative-energy state can temporarily escape to a positive-energy state, creating thereby an electron – hole pair. After a while the electron would return to the negative-energy state, "plugging the hole". Alternatively, one could say the electron and the positron annihilate each other. The point simply is that the vacuum is restless, and pair formation followed by annihilation is rather like water being tossed up by the sea waves, which later returns to the sea. The practical consequences of such vacuum fluctuations are two-fold. Consider a free electron. Due to the vacuum fluctuations, its mass is changed by an amount Δm_{vF}; this is one effect. The second is that the charge is altered by an amount Δe.

How do we know all this is true? Because these effects leave unmistakable finger prints in various experiments, as will be pointed out in Chapter 3. Please note that the fluctuations themselves cannot be observed; but their *effects* can be.

Much was expected from QED II but when infinities cropped up, everyone was depressed: In. 1936, Dirac said, "We may give it [QED

II] up without regrets—in fact because of its extreme complexity, most physicists will be glad to see the end of it."

1.8 The pre-war situation

The situation around 1939, i.e., just before the outbreak of World War II was one of near desperation. In fact, unable to fight the infinities, many drifted to other areas of physics, particularly nuclear physics. Much later Weisskopf recalled:

> The theory [QED II] was so ugly! All these absurd ideas and this terribly complicated mathematics, and it all looked very ugly. In a sense, I suppose the problem [of the infinities] seemed academic because for a long time nobody knew where the physics was in it. And a lot of people just said, "To hell with it, I'm going to do some nuclear physics".

The main problem was that people did not have a clear idea of the different ways in which divergence could arise. Weisskopf had drawn attention to vacuum polarisation as a source of trouble. There were other sources of divergences also but these had not been clearly identified; nor how they conspired in combination in different physical phenomena. The pity is that a few people like Serber and Dancoff came close to successfully cancelling the infinities but didn't quite make it. It was much later, in 1948, when the answer emerged from the work of Feynman and others that the early workers like Weisskopf, Serber and Dancoff realised how they had the solution nearly within their grasp.

Now a little story belonging to that period. At that time, Dirac who was on a round-the-world trip passed through America. He made a stop over in California where his host was Oppenheimer (you will meet him in a later chapter). Oppenheimer asked his junior associates including Serber to discuss with Dirac what they were doing to kill the infinities. Delighted by the opportunity, Serber and his colleagues spent over an hour explaining their work. Throughout, Dirac remained silent. After the presentation was over, Serber expected Dirac to ask questions, make comments or say something. Nothing happened; dead silence prevailed. Finally Dirac said, "Where is the Post office?" Serber was taken aback. But picking up courage Serber accompanied Dirac to the Post office, hoping to elicit comments on the way but Dirac offered none; Frustrated, Serber asked Dirac point blank whether he had any comments. Dirac replied, "I can't do two things at once." Serber was demolished and took a long time to recover!

1.9 A recap

Let us now take stock, which we do with the help of Fig. 1.2. To start with, Dirac in 1927 brought non-relativistic QM and the quantum theory of radiation together in QED I. It was a useful beginning, and in fact QED I is still used by students and engineers. Later Dirac proposed his relativistic equation for the electron, whose interpretation went through a phase of evolution, culminating in the hole

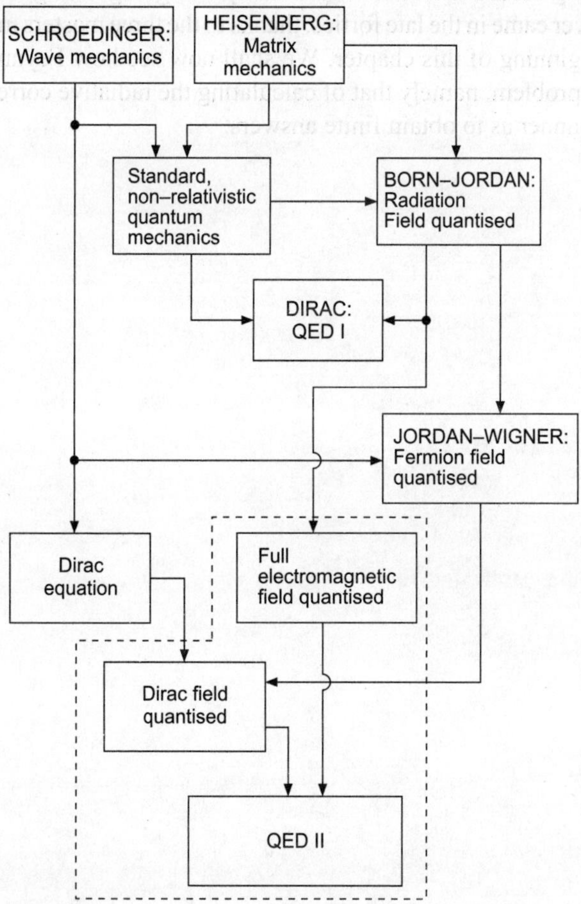

Fig.1.2 Flow chart showing the evolution of QED I and QED II.

theory and all that. Then came the Dirac field and its second quantisation (see also Box 1.2). Meanwhile the entire electromagnetic field (i.e., not only the transverse fields describing radiation but also the longitudinal field describing electrostatic interaction) was quantised, and soon the two fields were linked together in one unified framework—the result was QED II. All these developments which were due to the combined efforts of many are gathered together in the dotted box in Fig. 1.2. QED II was supposed to be what the doctor ordered, but it proved quite disappointing by throwing up a lot of unwanted infinities.

So where was the problem? Relativity had been duly respected and the electromagnetic field had been treated with proper care. And yet one was getting absurd answers. What exactly was going wrong and where? The answer came in the late forties, thanks to the three masters mentioned at the beginning of this chapter. We shall now see how Feynman dealt with the problem, namely that of calculating the radiative corrections in such a manner as to obtain finite answers.

Appendix to Chapter 1

This appendix is for the more technically minded, ft offers a bird's-eye view of the so-called gauge business in electromagnetic theory. Before I get on to that, a few remarks about field quantisation. I would like to introduce the topic by considering the *phonon* field.

Phonon is a new word, and I should explain what it stands for. Consider a one-dimensional chain of atoms as in figure (a). Adjacent atoms are coupled by (harmonic) springs. When all the atoms are at rest, the spacings between the atoms is the same and one has a perfect, one-dimensional crystal. If the atoms are disturbed, i.e., displaced from their equilibrium positions, elastic energy would be stored in the lattice due to the various springs being compressed and dilated as the case may be. This then translates into kinetic energy and the lattice begins to jiggle. No matter how complicated the jiggling pattern, it can always be built up by a suitable superposition of basic lattice vibrational patterns called *normal modes*. Essentially they are waves propagating along the atomic chain, each wave being characterised by a frequency ν and a wave vector $k(= 2\pi/\lambda)$. For light and sound waves, we have the familiar relation $\nu\lambda =$ constant, the constant being the speed of light or sound as the case may be. For lattice vibrational waves, however, there is no such constancy, but that does not matter.

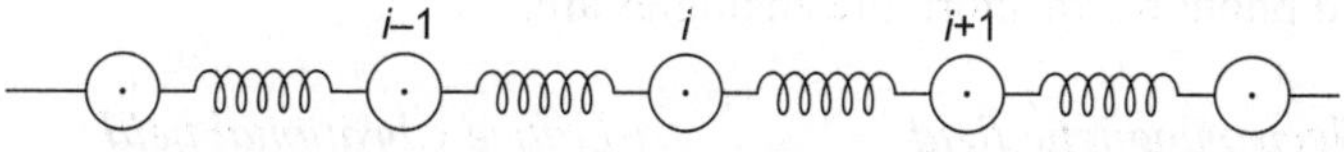

(a)

Let η_i be the displacement of the ith atom from its equilibrium position—see Fig. (b).

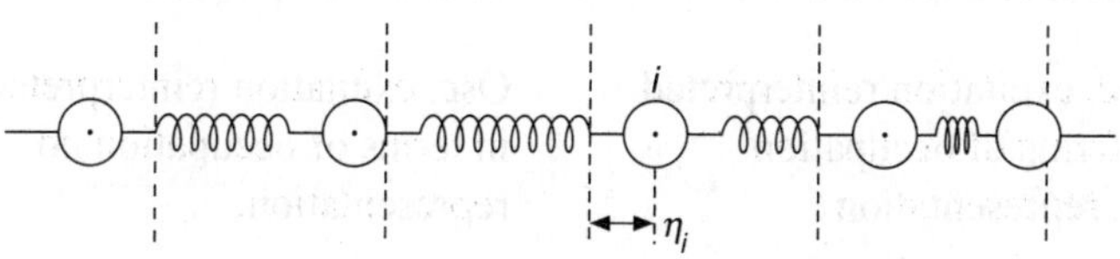

(b)

The energy or rather the Hamiltonian of the atomic chain can be written as

$$H = \frac{1}{2m}\sum_i \left\{ \pi_i^2 + K\left(\eta_{i+1} - \eta_i\right)^2 \right\}. \quad (1)$$

Here m is the mass of the atom, π_i the momentum and K the spring constant. H can also be expressed in terms of the normal-mode parameters as

$$H = \sum_i \left(p_s^2 + \omega_s^2 q_s^2 \right). \quad (2)$$

Here $\omega_s = 2\pi v_s$ where v_s is the frequency of the s th normal mode. (q_s, p_s) denote respectively the (generalised) coordinate and momentum of the normal mode. Thanks to (2) one can now forget about the individual atoms and what they do.

So far, everything is classical. Transition to QM is made by regarding each normal-mode oscillator as a quantum oscillator. Remember, this is a fictitious oscillator. Corresponding to the frequency v_s the normal-mode oscillator would have energy levels at $(n + 1/2)hv_s$, $n = 0, 1, 2, \ldots$ I am sure you are beginning to see parallels with the radiation case. Indeed, the normal-mode oscillator excited to level n can equally well be thought of in terms of n vibrational quanta. It is these which are called phonons. In short, the analogies are:

Electromagnetic field	*Lattice vibrational field*
Electromagnetic wave	Vibrational wave
Equivalent oscillator	Equivalent oscillator
Osc. levels quantised	Osc. levels quantised
Osc. excitation reinterpreted in terms of occupation no. representation	Osc. excitation reinterpreted in terms of occupation no. representation.
Quanta called phonons	Quanta called photons
Photons can exist in free space	Phonons exist only inside the crystal

Once the phonons have been introduced, one can completely forget the lattice and deal with the equivalent gas of (non-interacting) phonons, at least as far as many properties of the crystal are concerned, e.g., thermal.

We now turn to the electromagnetic field. In the lab, what we deal with are the electric and magnetic fields E and H; these are the practical manifestations of the field. As you are aware, radiation is described in terms of transverse electromagnetic waves. They have, associated with them, only four degrees of freedom. The classical equations which describe the behaviour of E and H are first-order partial differential equations—the famous Maxwell's equations. But for describing wave propagation, one prefers wave equations which are second-order partial differential equations. The wave equations are more conveniently described in terms of two other quantities A and ϕ referred to respectively as the vector and scalar potentials. Notice that A and ϕ also together make up four degrees of freedom. Naturally, A and ϕ determine E and H, but we must remember that only the latter are physically observable.

How does one choose A and ϕ ? This is an interesting question because it turns out that many different choices of the pair (A, ϕ) are possible which lead to the *same* (E, H). There is therefore some freedom in the choice of the former; this is called *gauge* freedom.

The word gauge occurs frequently in QED and even more so in high-energy physics; in fact it comes in various combinations like gauge transformations, gauge in variance and so forth. It all sounds very mysterious and fashionable but don't get worried. The word gauge was first introduced into physics by the mathematical physicist Hermann Weyl. In workshops, mechanics use steel blocks of fixed sizes for checking lengths etc.; these are referred to as gauge blocks. Roughly speaking therefore, gauge simply means a reference size or length (recall broad gauge, metre gauge and narrow gauge in our railways). Choosing a particular pair (A, ϕ) is referred to as choosing a gauge or gauge fixing. Two gauge choices popularly employed are the *Lorentz* gauge and the *Coulomb* gauge; the latter is also sometimes referred to as the *transverse* gauge. A change of gauge is referred to as gauge transformation. While gauge choice might be made on the basis of convenience, the final physical result must of course be independent of such choices, i.e., it must be *gauge invariant*. In QED there is a double responsibility—not only must the theory be relativistically covariant but also gauge invariant.

In formal theory, one deals with A and ϕ rather than E and H. In fact A and ϕ are combined into a single vector with four components, as is the practice in relativity. Quantising the electromagnetic field boils down then to writing suitable commutation relations for the components of this four vector.

A flow chart providing an overview is given in figure (c).

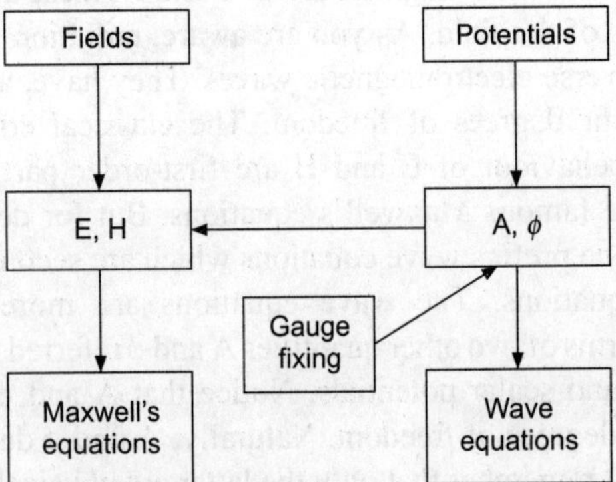

(c)

Perhaps the most important point you have to absorb from all this is: In quantum field theory, every (type of) particle is an excitation of some particular field and, conversely, with every field we can associate particles of definite mass and spin.

2 Saying It With Pictures

> At last, we had a quantum theory of electricity and magnetism with which we could calculate.
>
> *Feynman*

2.1 Introduction

This chapter is devoted to Feynman's approach to QED. Feynman not only cracked the problem of the infinities but more importantly, he introduced a fresh approach in QM. As Dyson puts it,

> Feynman's approach was the most original of the three [i.e., Tomonaga, Schwinger and Feynman]: he was willing to take nothing for granted, and so he was forced to reconstruct the whole of quantum mechanics and electrodynamics from his own point of view.

Let us now hear Feynman speak about it:

> The Schroedinger equation
>
> $$i\hbar\left(\partial\psi/\partial t\right)=H\psi \tag{2.1}$$
>
> describes the change in the infinitesimal wave function ψ in an infinitesimal time step Δt as due to the operation of an operator $\exp\left(-iH\,\Delta t/\hbar\right)$. One can ask also, if $\psi(x_1, t_1)$ is the wave function at x_1 at time t_1, what is the wave function at time $t_2 > t_1$?

Feynman writes the answer as

$$\psi\left(x_2,t_2\right)=\int K\left(x_2,t_2;x_1,t_1\right)\psi\left(x_1,t_1\right)d^3x_1. \tag{2.2}$$

Equation (2.2) is just a recipe for calculating $\psi(x_2, t_2)$ given $\psi(x_1, t_1)$.

The difference in the philosophies underlying (2.1) and (2.2) must be appreciated. In the former case one arrives at $\psi(x_2, t_2)$ in a long sequence of successive, infinitesimal steps whereas in the latter case one takes "a giant leap forward" with the help of the *kernel K*. It is to visualise this process that Feynman introduced diagrams which are now referred to as *Feynman diagrams*. Essentially they are world lines, and they have revolutionised practical, field-theoretic calculations. At one stage, Feynman had his car painted all over with such diagrams! So popular is the diagrammatical method that Schwinger once remarked, "Like the ubiquitous silicon chip ..., the Feynman diagram was bringing computation to the masses."

In QED (Feynman's version that is), one is basically interested in the world lines of the particles concerned, i.e., electrons. During its journey the electron may do one or more of the following:

1. Propagate freely;
2. interact with a radiation field;
3. interact with other electrons;
4. interact with an external field.

The basic process intrinsic to all the above is the interaction of an electron with a photon; this would become clear shortly.

Historically, Feynman first introduced his new approach for non-relativistic QM. He derived inspiration for it from a paper published by Dirac in 1933, in which he [Dirac] sought to construct a quantum theory based on the Lagrangian approach to classical mechanics. Later Feynman made everything pukka by extending his work to the relativistic case also. This was achieved by dealing with the Dirac field on the one hand and using a properly quantised electromagnetic field on the other. Naturally all this involves a lot of technicalities but fortunately (!) they are beyond our scope; the underlying principles, however, are not too difficult to grasp.

2.2 About Feynman diagrams

From now on, this chapter would revolve largely around Feynman diagrams. No matter how complicated they are, they can all be regarded as built up from the basic module shown in Fig. 2.1. Here the solid line shows the electron and the wavy line the photon. In words, the figure says that the electron in going from (x_1, t_1) to (x_2, t_2) interacts with the electromagnetic field at (x_A, t_A).

Notation: It is somewhat tiring to write (x_1, t_1), (x_A, t_A), (x_2, t_2), etc. Instead we shall merely write 1, A, 2, ... etc. Each symbol is a shorthand notation for a space-time point.

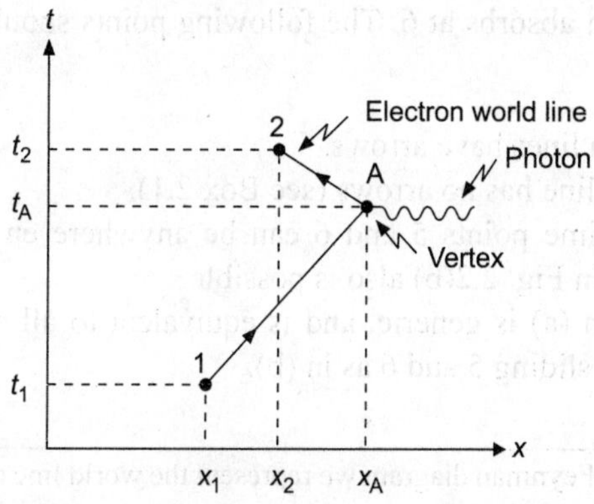

Fig.2.1 The solid line is the world line of the electron as it goes from (x_1, t_1) to (x_2, t_2). At (x_A, t_A), there is an interaction with a photon. The wavy line shows the photon, and the vertex the basic interaction between the electron and the electromagnetic field.

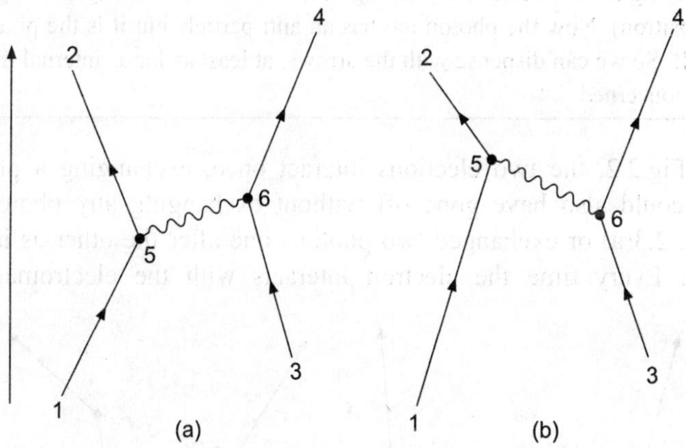

Fig.2.2 Feynman diagram for $e - e$ scattering, (a) and (b) are two alternate scenarios in which events 5 and 6 have different time orderings.

Using the basic scheme of Fig. 2.1, let us draw a picture for the interaction between two electrons. This is shown in Fig. 2.2(a). There are two electrons, one of which goes from 1 to 3 and the other from 2 to 4. En route, the first electron emits a photon at 5 which the second electron absorbs at 6. The following points should be carefully noted:

1. The electron lines have arrows.
2. The photon line has no arrows (see Box 2.1).
3. The space-time points 5 and 6 can be anywhere en route. Thus a scenario as in Fig. 2.2(b) also is possible.
4. The diagram (a) is generic, and is equivalent to all other diagrams obtained by sliding 5 and 6 as in (b).

Box 2.1 In a Feynman diagram we represent the world line of an electron with a straight line and that of the photon with a wavy line. The electron has an anti-particle namely the positron, if we explicitly take note of the positron, then we must have separate world lines for them. But Feynman does not bring in the positron. Instead he says that an electron going back in time represents a positron. So arrows have to be attached to the electron world line to show whether the electron is moving forward in time (i.e., behaving as an electron) or moving back-ward in time (i.e., behaving as a positron). Now the photon too has an anti-particle but it is the photon itself. So we can dispense with the arrows, at least as far as internal lines are concerned.

In Fig.2.2, the two elections interact once, exchanging a photon. They could also have gone off without exchanging any photons as in Fig. 2.3(a) or exchanged two photons one after the other as in Fig. 2.3(b). Every time the electron interacts with the electromagnetic

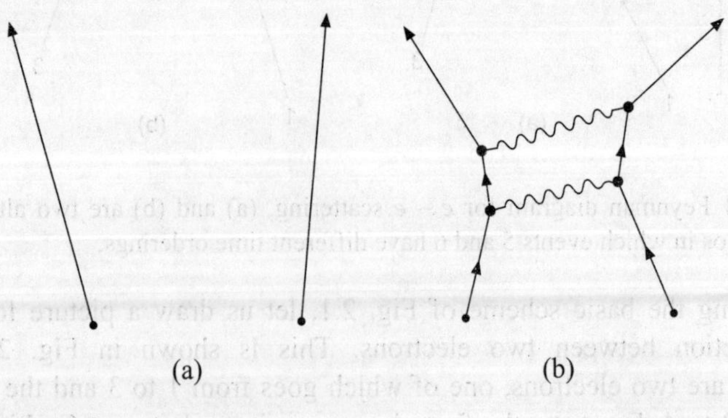

Fig.2.3 Electron – electron scattering again, (a) with no exchange of virtual photons and (b) with two such exchanges.

field, i.e., every time there is a perturbation due to the electromagnetic field there appears a junction or vertex in the diagram. The number of vertices depends on the order of the perturbation. Thus in Fig. 2.3(b) the perturbation acts four times and the diagram is therefore relevant in fourth-order perturbation theory.

2.3 Some practice with diagrams

Let us now try to get some more feel for and practice with Feynman diagrams by drawing them for a few physical processes. We start with electron – photon scattering (Compton effect) for which there are two diagrams in the lowest-order; these are shown in Fig. 2.4. Notice that the two are not equivalent because in one case the electron of momentum p_1 interacts with the photon of momentum $\hbar k_1$ whereas in the other case it interacts with the photon whose momentum is $\hbar k_2$. Both processes are possible and must be allowed for. In the experiment, we see only the initial and the final states and have no means of knowing what happens in the intermediate state shown between the dotted lines. Processes which happen in the intermediate state are referred to as *virtual processes*. They are *not* directly observable in experiments but their effects can be detected.

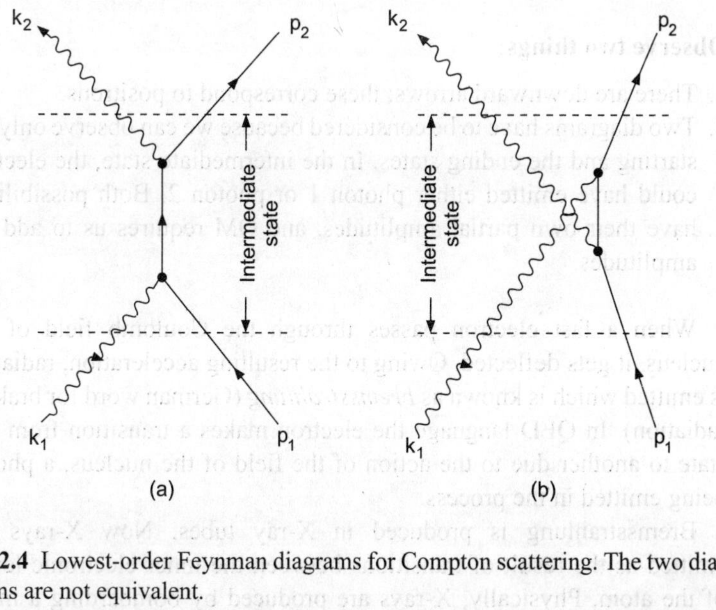

Fig.2.4 Lowest-order Feynman diagrams for Compton scattering. The two diagrams are not equivalent.

We consider next the annihilation of an electron – positron pair. As you know this results in the emission of two photons going roughly in opposite directions. There are two Feynman diagrams which describe this process in the lowest-order; these are shown in Fig. 2.5.

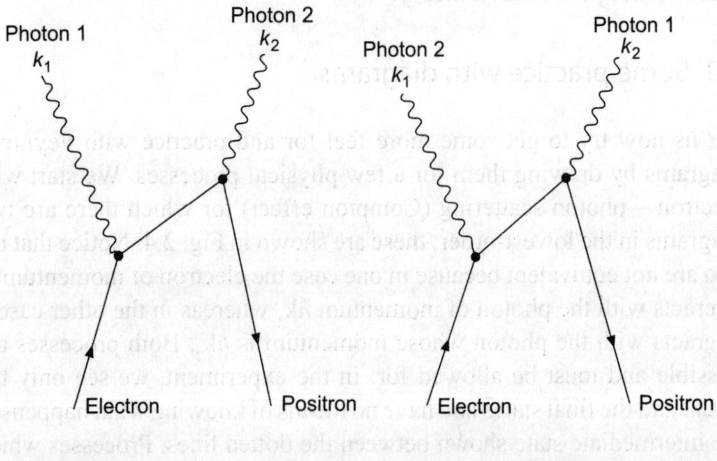

Fig.2.5 Feynman diagram for electron – positron annihilation. Two possibilities with photons 1 and 2 interchanged are shown. Experimentally, one cannot distinguish between the two. QM therefore requires that the partial amplitudes for the two be superposed.

Observe two things:

1. There are downward arrows; these correspond to positrons.
2. Two diagrams have to be considered because we can observe only the starting and the ending states. In the intermediate state, the electron could have emitted either photon 1 or photon 2. Both possibilities have their own partial amplitudes, and QM requires us to add the amplitudes.

When a fast electron passes through the Coulomb field of the nucleus, it gets deflected. Owing to the resulting acceleration, radiation is emitted which is known as *bremsstrahlung* (German word for braking radiation). In QED language the electron makes a transition from one state to another due to the action of the field of the nucleus, a photon being emitted in the process.

Bremsstrahlung is produced in X-ray tubes. Now X-rays are emitted as the result of transitions between the inner electronic levels of the atom. Physically, X-rays are produced by bombarding a metal target (of say copper or tungsten) with a beam of fast electrons. Some of the incident electrons do produce such atomic transitions resulting in the emission of sharp lines as in Fig. 2.6(a) but many other electrons simply produce bremsstrahlung radiation. As a result the spectrum of the radiation coming from the tube is a composite one as in Fig. 2.6(b). In the lowest order, the bremsstrahlung process is described by the two diagrams in Fig. 2.7.

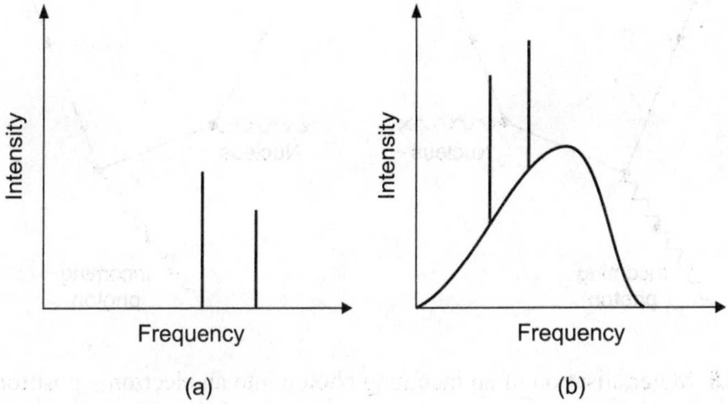

Fig.2.6 Intensity of X-rays emitted as a function of frequency, (a) shows the spectrum if one considers only transitions between inner atomic levels. The observed spectrum from a X-ray tube is shown in (b). It is a superposition of the line spectrum and bremsstrahlung.

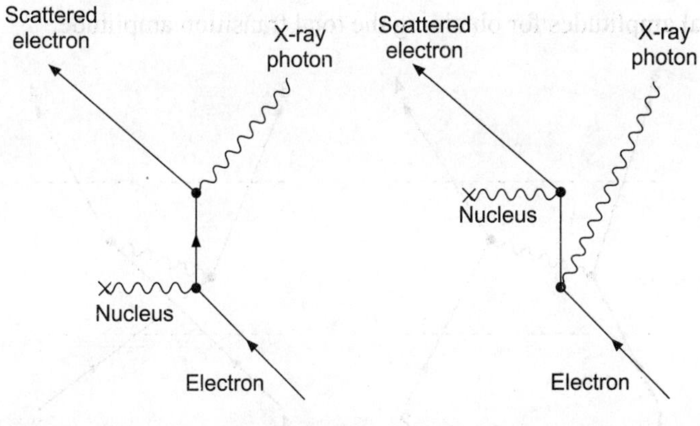

Fig.2.7 Lowest-order Feynman diagrams associated with bremsstrahlung. The interaction of the electron with the nucleus is shown by a wavy line ending in a cross.

Earlier I discussed the annihilation of an electron – positron pair. The reverse process in which a photon produces a pair is also possible. For conserving momentum, the photon requires the assistance of a "spectator" which is usually a nucleus. The lowest-order diagrams are shown in Fig. 2.8.

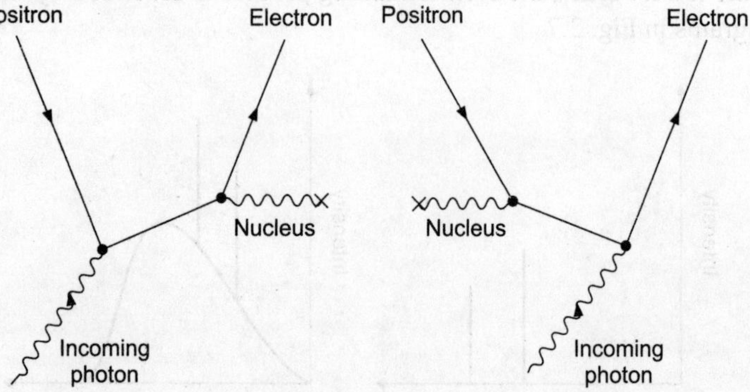

Fig.2.8 Materialisation of an incoming photon into an electron – positron pair. For conserving momentum, a spectator, e.g., a nucleus, is necessary. Interaction with the latter is shown by a wavy line ending in a cross.

Electron – electron scattering has already been mentioned a couple of times. Two diagrams as in Fig. 2.9 are relevant to this case. Once again two diagrams are necessary because we cannot say which of the two possibilites occurs in the intermediate state and as usual we must add the partial amplitudes for obtaining the total transition amplitude.

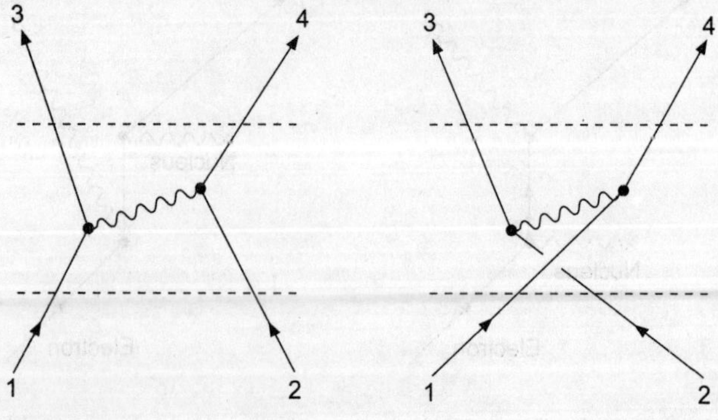

Fig.2.9 Two lowest-order diagrams pertinent to *e* – *e* scattering.

2.4 The effect of perturbations on the kernel

Let us go back to equation (2.2), the role of the kernel, and how perturbation theory is employed.

The electron kernel $K(2, 1)$ essentially "carries" the particle from 1 to 2. If the particle is free, we write the kernel as $K^{(0)}(2,1)$ whereas if it has had interactions on the way, we write the kernel as $K(2,1)$. The extent to which K is different from $K^{(0)}$ depends upon how many times the particle is perturbed along the journey from 1 to 2. Some examples of perturbation have been given in the Feynman diagrams presented earlier.

Of what use is the kernel K? Remember, ultimately we want to make contact with experiment which means we want to calculate an appropriate matrix element and thereafter its modulus squared. If $\psi(1)$ and $\psi(2)$ denote the initial and final states, the desired element is

$$\langle\psi(2)|K(2,1)|\psi(1)\rangle \sim \int \psi^*(2)K(2,1)\psi(1)d^3x_1d^3x_2. \tag{2.3}$$

Let us now look at the perturbation business a bit more closely. At the practical level, we shall have to consider (i) perturbation due to the electromagnetic field, and (ii) perturbation due to an external potential. The usual symbols for these are A and V respectively. For the present, let us consider a generic perturbation U which can act 0, 1, 2, ... times in succession. The effect of this on $K^{(0)}$ can thus be written:

$$K(2,1) = K^{(0)}(2,1) + K^{(1)}(2,1) + K^{(2)}(2,1) + \ldots \tag{2.4}$$

Here,

$$K^{(1)}(2,1) = \text{constant} \int K^{(0)}(2,3)U(3)K^{(0)}(3,1)dt_3d^3x_3, \tag{2.5}$$

and denotes the first-order contribution. We shall write this schematically as

$$K^{(1)}(2,1) = K^{(0)}(2,3)U(3)K^{(0)}(3,1). \tag{2.6}$$

Essentially, we have avoided writing the integration over 3 which, as you will notice, occurs repeatedly on the right-hand side of (2.5).

In his popular book on quantum electrodynamics entitled *QED*, Feynman employs a similar symbolic notation. Using our version, we can write the contributions in various successive orders as:

$$K^{(2)}(2,1) = K^{(0)}(2,4)U(4)K^{(0)}(4,3)U(3)K^{(0)}(3,1) \qquad (2.7)$$

$$K^{(3)}(2,1) = K^{(0)}(2,5)U(5)K^{(0)}(5,4)U(4)K^{(0)}(4,3) \times U(3)K^{(0)}(3,1), \text{ etc.} \qquad (2.8)$$

In the above, we have considered perturbations occurring to a single particle while on a jaunt from 1 to 2. Once again, we suppress writing the integrals over variables which repeat.

In a scattering problem (see Fig. 2.3), we would be interested in the simultaneous progress of two electrons. We now write the kernel as

$$K(3,4;1,2) = K^{(0)}(3,4;1,2) + K^{(1)}(3,4;1,2) + \text{ etc.} \qquad (2.9)$$

The first term on the right represents the case where the electrons do not exchange any photons (see Fig. 2.3(a)). It can be written as

$$K^{(0)}(3,4;1,2) = K^{(0)}(3,1)K^{(0)}(4,2). \qquad (2.10)$$

When the electrons exchange one photon (as in Fig. 2.2), we have

$$K^{(0)}(4,6)A(6)K^{(0)}(6,3)P(6,5)K^{(0)}(2,5)A(5)K^{(0)}(5,1) \qquad (2.11)$$

where $P(6,5)$ is the *photon kernel* and A the perturbation.

The above is an example of space-time representation of evolution and conveys the gist of the Feynman diagram which, I remind you once again, is really a space-time diagram. In practice, one wants to calculate matrix elements and all that. For this purpose, it is convenient to consider the electron and photon kernels in terms of the momenta carried by the electron and the photon respectively. Technically, this is done by rewriting formulae such as (2.11) in what is called the *momentum representation*. Given a Feynman diagram, there are clear-cut rules for expressing its content in the momentum representation. Simplifying the expression and evaluation is thereafter a matter of slogging. Figure 2.10 gives an example of the change in viewpoint called for when looking at things in terms of momenta. Obviously, the momenta of the electron and the photon can vary, and one must

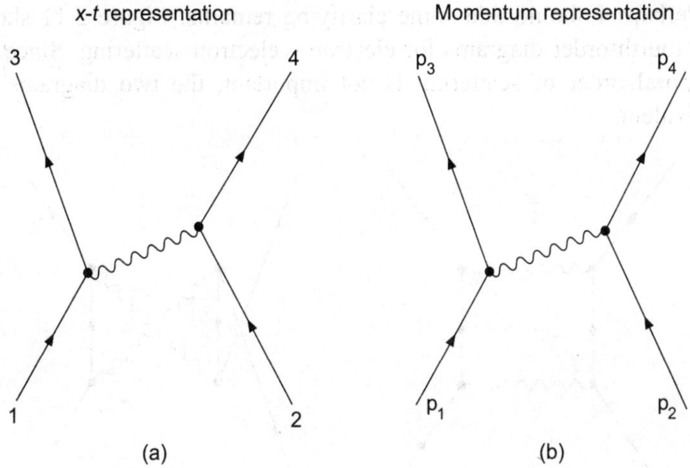

Fig.2.10 (a) shows the standard Feynman diagram made up of world lines, (b) is a schematic of (a) useful while discussing the momentum representation. The straight lines no longer have the significance of world lines.

allow for all possibilities, i.e., integrate over all momenta. The much-disliked infinities arise due to such integrations.

The meaning and purpose of drawing diagrams can now be explained. Firstly of course the diagrams enable a clear visualisation of the processes occurring in various orders of perturbation theory. Once the diagram is drawn, one goes over into the momentum representation and cranks the handle. Thus the drill in perturbation calculations is roughly as follows:

1. Draw all the topologically different diagrams corresponding. to a given order. In Fig. 2.2, the two diagrams are equivalent for the reason already mentioned. They are therefore not considered separately because the calculational scheme encompasses all such equivalent diagrams.
2. Diagrams demanded by the requirements of exchange process must be allowed for; e.g., recall Fig. 2.9.
3. Go now into the momentum representation and use the tool kit provided by Feynman.
4. Add the contributions from all the diagrams.

Perhaps I should add some clarifying remarks. Figure 2.11 shows two fourth-order diagrams for electron – electron scattering. Since the temporal order of scattering is not important, the two diagrams are equivalent.

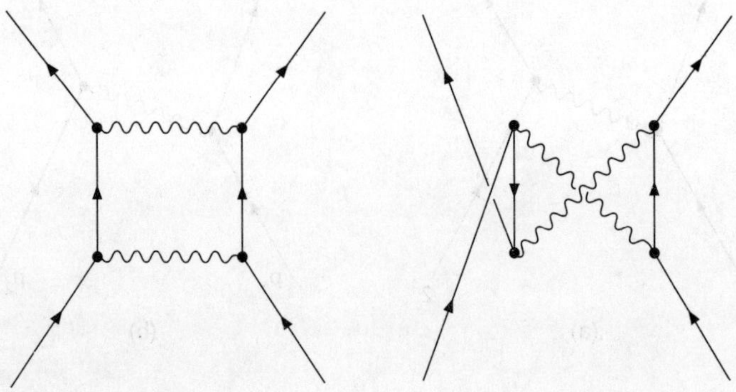

Fig.2.11 The fourth-order diagrams for $e - e$ scattering. The diagrams are equivalent

Consider now the diagrams in Fig. 2.12 which show the interaction of an electron with an external field (represented by a wavy line ending in a cross). Here Figs. 2.12(b) and (c) are both of third-order but they are not equivalent.

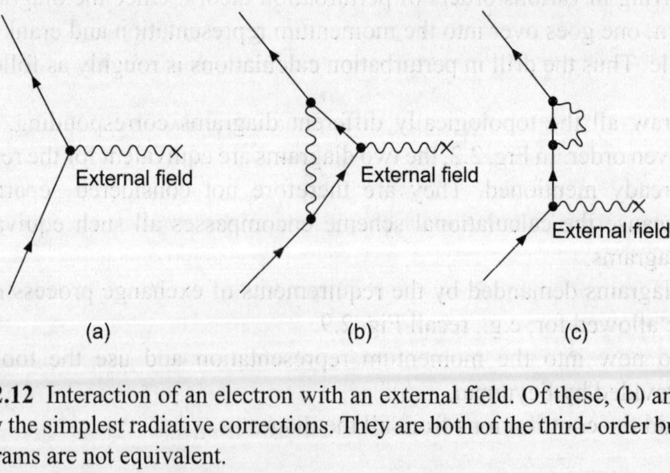

Fig.2.12 Interaction of an electron with an external field. Of these, (b) and (c) show the simplest radiative corrections. They are both of the third- order but the diagrams are not equivalent.

You should not get the impression that this stuff is easy. Drawing the diagram perhaps is but not so the use of the tool kit.

As Feynman once said during a popular lecture:

> In order to make any reasonable predictions with this new scheme of quantum electrodynamics, you have to draw a lot of diagrams. It takes seven years—four years undergraduate and three graduate—to train our students to do that in a tricky, efficient way.

Well, there you are!

2.5 Mass renormalisation

How does all this help in tackling the infinities? A few words now about that. Consider a free electron going from 1 to 2. Our first inclination would be to represent it by a Feynman diagram as in Fig. 2.13(a). But then, what we think is a free electron is not free in the true sense of the word because it is always interacting with its own field, giving rise to diagrams as in Fig. 2.13(b), (c), (d), etc. What we experimentally observe as a free electron is really a *bare* electron described by Fig. 2.13(a) *plus* all the *dressing* due to (b), (c), (d), etc. In other words, *we cannot ever observe a bare electron.*

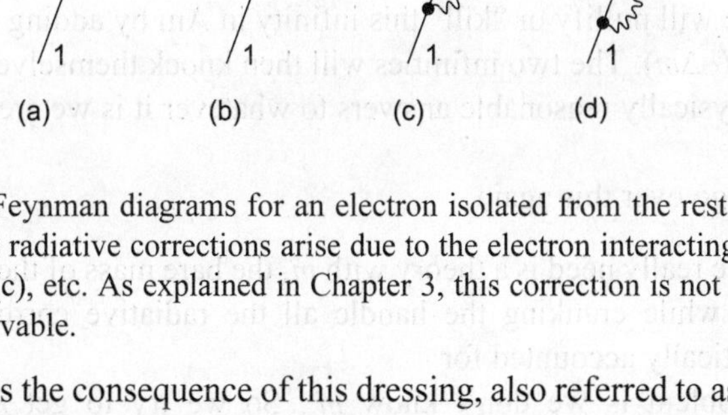

Fig.2.13 Feynman diagrams for an electron isolated from the rest of the universe. The radiative corrections arise due to the electron interacting with itself as in (b), (c), etc. As explained in Chapter 3, this correction is not experimentally observable.

What is the consequence of this dressing, also referred to as *radiative correction*? According to standard QM, if E is the energy of a free particle, the wave function would change in time as

$$\psi(t) = e^{-iEt/\hbar}\psi(0), \tag{2.12}$$

i.e., time evolution merely adds a phase factor $e^{-iEt/\hbar}$. We don't expect the "dressing" business to change the basic story, except to alter E to $(E + \Delta E)$ say. In turn, it is as if the mass of the particle has changed from m_0 the value appropriate to a bare particle, to $(m_0 + \Delta m)$, the value appropriate to the dressed or *physically observed* isolated particle (which we are used to calling as free). From relativity, $\Delta m = \Delta E/c^2$.

So far so good. Trouble starts when one tries to calculate Δm because the answer comes out to be infinity. This is bad news because we know that for the electron $(m_0 + \Delta m)$ has been measured and found to be $\sim 9.1 \times 10^{-28}$ gm, a finite number. Let us represent this as m_{exp}. If Δm is infinite but $m_{exp} = (m_0 + \Delta m)$ is a finite number, then it implies m_0 is infinite. Things are now getting from bad to worse because to obtain the observed mass, we perhaps have to subtract one infinity from another!

All this leads to yet another difficulty. Let us say we want to solve the hydrogen atom problem. With the good old Schroedinger equation, we would, without any hesitation, use the value 9.1×10^{-28} gm for the mass of the electron. In QED, we cannot quite do this because the experimental mass includes the effect of dressing. On the other hand, the effect of dressing is what we wish to calculate. So what we need as input is m_0 but that is infinity, and it is embarassing to do theory with an infinity staring in our face.

This difficulty has been realised for a long time, almost from the time the Dirac equation was proposed. To overcome it a new strategy was required which is what Tomonaga, Schwinger and Feynman provided. They said (effectively): "Let us do whatever calculation we want using $m_0 + \Delta m$. Don't worry if this means tucking in an infinity in the shape of Δm. We will nullify or "kill" this infinity in Am by adding a counter term with $(-\Delta m)$. The two infinities will then knock themselves out and give us physically reasonable answers to whatever it is we are trying to calculate."

Let me go over this again.

1. What we really need is a theory with m_0 the bare mass of the election, so that while cranking the handle all the radiative correction are automatically accounted for.
2. The problem is we don't know m_0. So we try to get m_0 in the following way. We consider an isolated electron. Its bare mass is m_0. We allow the election to interact with its own radiation field. Calculation shows that the mass now increase to $(m_0 + \Delta m)$. We in fact expect $(m_0 + \Delta m)$ to be equal to 9.1×10^{-28} gm, the observed mass m_{exp}. Unfortunately Δm turns out to be ∞. So

we have no hope of comparing $(m_0 + \Delta m)$ with mexp and arriving at m_0 by subtracting Δm. If we try to do that, we would find $m_0 = -\infty$!

3. We seem to be stumped; so, let us go back to what we need. To be specific, let us say we need a theory for the hydrogen atom, in which case, starting with the bare electron and then switching on (i) the interaction of the electron with its own radiation field and (ii) the interaction of the electron with the proton, we can calculate the energy levels of the atom. Such a calculation would include all radiative corrections. Unfortunately, we are unable to proceed because we don't know m_0.
4. Instead, let us tackle the hydrogen atom problem differently by assuming a mass $(m_0 + \Delta m)$ for the electron and then switching on both the coulombic and radiative interactions.
5. You would howl, " Objection ! You are then including radiation effects twice, once implicitly in writing $(m_0 + \Delta m)$ and the second time explicitly." You are right !
6. So we now do something clever. In the second step, we don't quite use the interaction H_I but $(H_I - \Delta m)$ This way, the infinity implied by the use of the mass $(m_0 + \Delta m)$ is cancelled by the term $(-\Delta m)$ in $(H_I - \Delta m)$.
7. Thus, what we really end up with is the *difference* between the self-energy effects of an isolated electron and an electron bound in a hydrogen atom. This *difference* is calculable and also measurable. So we not only have something to latch on to but also to test.

The process of replacing mo by $m_0 + \Delta m$ in the starting framework is referred to as *mass renormalisation*.

2.6 How the counter-term works

Perhaps I should add a few more words of explanation. We start with a bare particle described by H_0 and represented by the diagram in Fig. 2.14(a) (the appropriate mass would naturally be m_0 Say the contribution is A. With radiative corrections, the result say is $(A + B)$. We now switch on the external potential H_c and ignore radiative corrections for a moment. This leads to a contribution C say; and with dressing effects, there is an increase D. There is no reason why D should equal B; correspondingly, the mass increase $\Delta m'$ (say) need not equal Δm (associated with B). If now we use the counter-term technique, the situation is as in Fig. 2.14(e). The infinity in D is countered by that in B to deliver a finite result; this is the spirit of changing m_0 to $m_0 + \Delta m$ (i.e., renormalisation), and following it by the use of the counter-term. When we let $H_c \to 0$, we find (see Fig 2.14(f)).

$$C + D - B \to A + B - B = A,$$

which is as it should be. See also Box 2.2.

> **Box 2.2** I don't want you to think that there is any hocus-pocus in this infinity subtraction business. It is not as if one is trying to calculate $(\infty - \infty)$. Rather, one has $(X - Y)$, where X and Y both diverge to infinity. Now, divergence can be of many kinds like x^n $(n \geq 1)$, $\log x$ etc. Here x is a variable which $\to \infty$. The trouble maker is X, and one wants to nullify its effects with the counter term Y. So Y is carefully tailored to have the *same* divergence characteristic as X. The cancellation of infinities is then legitimate, safe and effective.

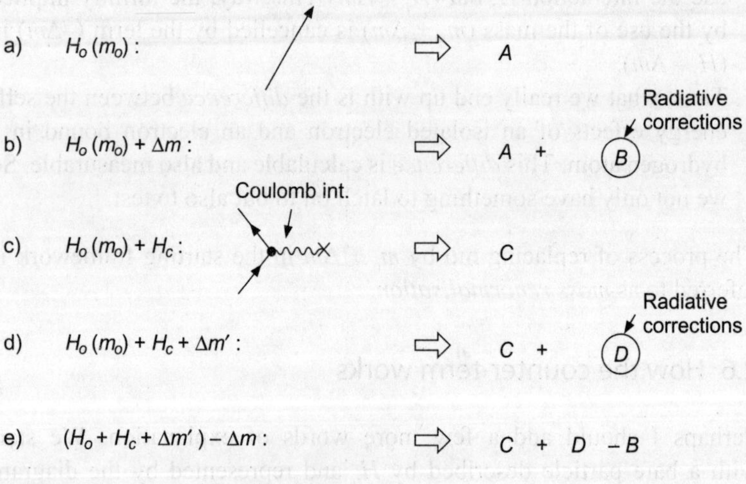

Fig.2.14 Schematic illustration of the role of the counter term. Explanations in text.

2.7 Meaning of renormalisation

The term renormalisation occurs frequently in QED and therefore deserves some explanation. An analogy might help. In the old days—I mean sixty or seventy years ago—salaries dit not include dearness allowance (DA). So, when prices of commodities started going up people clamoured for a "higher salary. The Government was clever (at least it thought it was!) and said: "No salary increase but we will give you an allowance called DA related to price increase." The employees only wanted money and did not care under what label it was given. As far as they were concerned, the pay packet was bigger, in tune with price increase. We have here an example of readjustment of earnings or pay-packet renormalisation if you like.

You might wonder: "But prices keep rising and the Government is forced to periodically jack up the DA. Do similar things happen in QED?" Good question because this brings up the problem of the *running coupling constant* to which I shall come shortly.

Meanwhile, we had better appreciate that renormalisation which only means readjustment should not be confused with infinities. It is true we are talking of both in the same breath but the two are different. Renormalisation is like the readjustments passengers make in a crowded railway compartment, as more and more passengers sqeeze in. Only, in QED renormalisation is a necessary prelude for battling infinities.

2.8 The cutoff business

Let us now look at Δm a bit more closely which we do by considering the diagram in Fig. 2.15. Focus on the photon emitted at 3 and

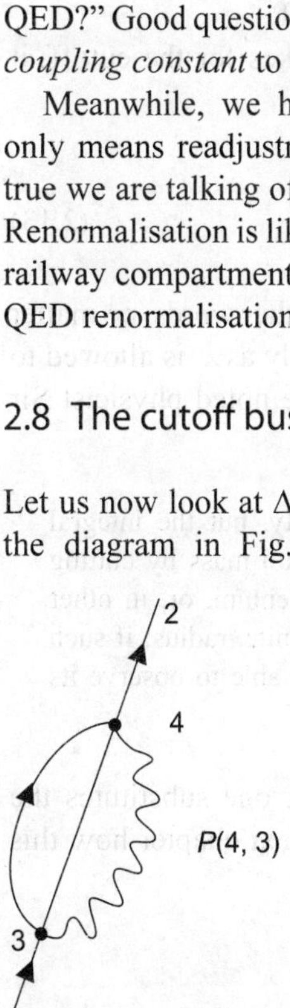

Fig.2.15 The simplest self-energy diagram for an isolated electron. The virtual photon denoted by the propagator $P(4,3)$ could be associated with any wave vector between 0 and ∞. Divergence arises when one integrates over all of them.

absorbed at 4 and described by $P(4,3)$. As I told you earlier, while using the tool kit one goes over into the momentum representation. In this case it means we must assign a value for $\hbar k$ the momentum of the photon. The question is, what value? It is clear the momentum could be anything which means one must integrate over all k to obtain the answer. But if the wave vector k is allowed to range from 0 to ∞, Δm comes out as ∞. Careful examination reveals that trouble is caused by photons with large value of k, i.e., the high-frequency photons.

At this stage one uses commonsense and argues that photons with $k > k_c$ or $\lambda < \lambda_c$ ($\lambda = 2\pi/k$), are "sluggish", i.e., they do not make a significant contribution. The wavelength λ_c is a cutoff; usually, it is taken to be the Compton wavelength—see section 1.7. Physically, the above argument is equivalent to supposing that the photon and the electron do not come closer than λ_c. This assumption is OK unless one considers very high energy processes (which one does not do here). The wave vector k_c or the equivalent length λ_c represents a practical cutoff.

Ignoring for a moment the actual value one takes for the cutoff, it turns out

$$\Delta m \sim m_0 \cdot \frac{3}{2\pi} \cdot \frac{e^2}{\hbar c} \log\left(\frac{M_c}{m_0}\right) + \frac{1}{4} \tag{2.13}$$

where $M_c = (\hbar/c\lambda_c)$ is called the *regulator mass*. In other words, no matter what the value of m_0 is, Δm diverges logarithmically as λ_c is allowed to become smaller and smaller (or as $M_c \to \infty$). The noted physicist Sir Rudolph Peierls comments:

> Of course, a logarithmic infinity, is still an infinity, but the integral could be made finite and comparable to real electron mass by cutting off the integration at some fantastically large momentum, or, in other words, giving the electron a fantastically small, if finite, radius; if such a cutoff really existed we would probably never be able to observe its consequences.

In practice, while making numerical calculations, one substitutes the Compton wavelength for λ_c. We shall see in the next chapter how this technology is used in computing the Lamb shift.

2.9 Charge renormalisation

Just as we have a problem with the bare mass of the electron, there is a similar problem in the case of the bare charge e_0. The charge e that we actually observe is a dressed charge, dressed by vacuum polarisation effects—see Fig. 2.16. In other words $e = e_0 + \Delta e$. If one tries to calculate Δe, one obtains infinity. So, as in the case of mass, one simply uses the experimental charge e in all practical calculations.

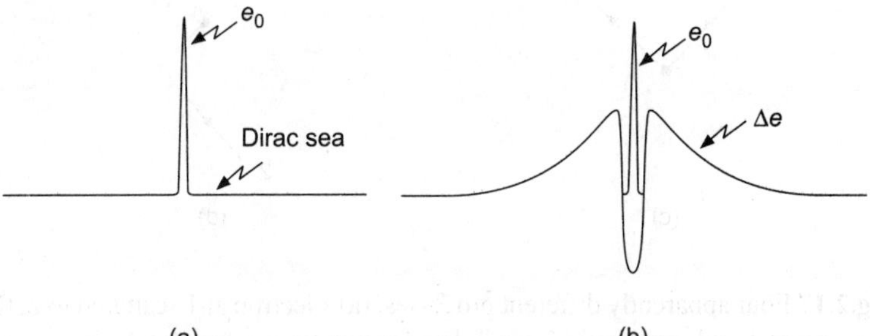

Fig.2.16 (a) Charge distribution in space due to a bare electron. This electron disturbs the vacuum, redistributing the (vacuum) charge as schematically shown in (b). Far away from the electron, one sees the net charge ($e_0 + \Delta e$) but getting very very close, one begins to see the bare charge itself.

You might wonder whether an extra counter-term is needed which is Associated with Δe, just as we had one earlier associated with Δm. The answer is no. The detailed reasons are quite technical (and I am not sure if I understand them!) but just take it that since Δm already includes effects due to vacuum polarisation, it covers up for Δe also; hence the introduction of another counter-term is not necessary.

2.10 Some fine print

There are some technicalities to which I would now like to draw your attention. Firstly, in Feynman's style of doing QED, only electrons are explicitly considered. We could, if we so desire, interpret electrons going back in time as positrons; that is our business. Thus in Fig. 2.17, there appear to be four different processes but in the Feynman picture all of them are encompassed into one formula.

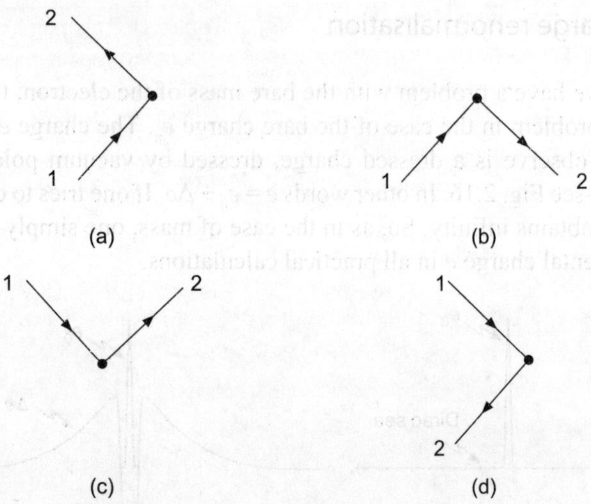

Fig.2.17 Four apparently different processes, (a) Electron at 1 scattered to 2. (b) Electron at 1 and positron at 2 annihilate leading to vacuum, (c) A single electron – positron pair created from the vacuum, (d) Positron at 2 scattered to 1. Probability for all processes are described by the same formula, i.e., $|K(2, 1)|^2$.

Our next remark is about the perturbation series. In this, one has typically an unperturbed Hamiltonian H_0 say and a perturbation term κH_I. Here κ is supposed to be a quantity small compared to unity. Therefore κH_I is small compared to H_0 and merits being called a small perturbation. The quantity κ is called a *coupling parameter* or *coupling coefficient*, and the perturbation expansion mentioned earlier is made to various orders in κ. And one also expects the corrections to decrease like $\kappa, \kappa_2, \kappa_3, \ldots$ (remember $\kappa < 1$).

In QED, the role of κ is played by $(e^2 / \hbar c) \sim (1/137)$. It is written as α and is referred to as the *fine structure constant.* (See also Box 2.3.) This brings us to our next point which is the possibility of the value of e changing due to vacuum polarisation. In a sense this is linked to the value for the quantity λ_c introduced earlier. If extremely high-energy processes are probed then λ_c would have to be extremely small. Under such circumstances, one would be seeing more and more of the bare charge e_0 (recall Fig. 2.16). The net effect is that e would appear to vary. If e varies, then so would the coupling constant α and if α increases we have to be concerned about the legitimacy of making a perturbation expansion. People have worried about this problem, and the news is that the expansion is quite safe and valid. The reason

Box 2.3 Quantum electrodynamics is the synthesis of quantum theory, electrodynamics and relativity. The fundamental constants representing these theories are $\hbar$, e and c respectively. In QED they come together as the fine-structure constant $\alpha = (e^2 / \hbar c) = 1/137$. All this you already know. This number (1/137) has intrigued people for a long time, and many are the stories connected with it. Here is one which involves the famous Wolfgang Pauli.

Pauli dies and goes to Heaven. In Heaven, God smiles at Pauli and says, "You have been a good man. I wish to reward you. Ask any question you like." Pauli immediately snaps: "Explain the fine structure constant." God nods and starts explaining. Pauli smiles and listens. After five minutes, he suddenly jumps up and shouts: "All that is completely wrong!"

Typical Pauli reaction in seminars!

is simply that for a to increase substantially over the value (~1/137), which is usually assumed, one must explore incredibly high-energy processes . These we need not bother about in cases like Lamb shift etc. On the other hand, when considering extremely high-energy processes, we might have to worry about the possible change in the coupling constant but then other forces (besides electromagnetic) enter the picture. At this stage the ball game changes completely, and plain old QED would no longer do.

The next point in the fine print category is the so-called *infra-red divergence*. Earlier I said that while taking into account the effect of photons of various momenta, we must assign a subdued role for those with high momenta (which we achieve by assigning them a regulator mass). The low frequency or low momenta photons do not give any problem, except those corresponding to $k = 0$ (zero frequency photons). This trouble crops up in scattering problems and is referred to as infra-red divergence. The trouble is more apparent than real and historically it arose because one was not sufficiently careful while dealing with the region near $k = 0$. Nowadays, one knows how to take care of the problem.

Perhaps you are wondering: "What about possible self-energy effects in the case of the photon? If the electron can acquire an electromagnetic mass due to dressing, what about the photon?" Experts have considered this issue and discovered that there are no self-energy effects to worry about in this case. The photon mass is simply zero—that's all there is to it.

2.11 A recap

Let us take stock. One might say: "It's all well to draw pictures but aren't you merely doing perturbation theory? What's so special about this way of book-keeping?" Good question, and the answer to this would be discussed in Chapter 4. Basically there are two things happening in this style of doing perturbation theory. First is that relativity is being respected at *every* stage of the calculation. A fancy way of saying this is that the "Feynman theory" is *manifestly covariant*; the meaning of this would be explained in Chapter 4. Secondly, gauge in variance is properly taken care of. The third point, and this is most important, is that renormalisation cum counter-term is built into the calculational procedure. By this I mean that one first identifies the source of infinities and then develops the calculational scheme in such a way that the trouble due to the infinities is kept in check. It is these three features—relativistic covariance, gauge invariance and renormalisation cum counter-term—which *together* deliver the goods.

I realise that all this may sound mysterious, besides being difficult to understand. Perhaps if I were to tell you how fantastic things happen as a result of this strategy, you might be more inclined to listen to the technical details behind this mystery. So on to the next chapter wherein I shall describe some of the early successes scored by QED III.

3 *The Acid Test*

> The theory of quantum electrodynamics has now lasted for more than forty years and has been tested more and more accurately over wider and wider range of conditions. At the present time I can proudly say there is no significant difference between experiment and theory!
>
> *Feynman*

3.1 Introduction

As you must have gathered from the previous two chapters, the foundation stone for QED as it exists today was laid by the early thirties. However, it was only in the forties that a strong effort was made towards constructing the superstructure. It all boiled down to developing a detailed Scheme of calculation in which relativity would be respected at each step, as also gauge invariance. This was the contribution that Tomonaga, Schwinger and Feynman independently made, almost at the same time. They did not discover any new law or new principle of physics; instead, they merely gave a comprehensive, and technically useful formalism for performing electro dynamical calculations. And yet their work not only created a stir at the time it was first announced but continues to be hailed even today. Why? An answer will be attempted in this chapter.

Earlier I remarked that QED has been affectionately referred to by Feynman as the jewel of physics. That is because QED predicts experimental results with an incredible accuracy that few theories of physics are able to match. Imagine predicting something to the sixth or seventh decimal place. To give an analogy, it is like specifying the distance from Kanyakumari to Delhi to within a couple of millimeters!

If QED had merely been a formalism, it would not have attracted so much attention as it did when it was first announced. What made it hit the headlines was its capacity to compute accurately certain experimental results which appeared in the late forties. There were three experimental observations which turned the tide. They are:

1. The Lamb shift in hydrogen.
2. The anomalous magnetic moment of the electron.
3. Splitting of the ground state of positronium.

A few words now about these important milestones.

3.2 The Lamb shift

Let us start with the spectrum of the hydrogen atom. Fig. 3.1(a) shows the energy levels in the simple Bohr model; we have already discussed this in Part I. We focus now on the low-lying levels and straightaway jump to the Dirac picture which is shown in Fig. 3.1(b). The level scheme is richer; as a result, what in the Bohr model would be a single spectral line due to the transition 2 → 1 now becomes a cluster of closely-spaced lines. To see these lines apart one needs a good spectrograph. The appearance of a cluster in place of a single line is referred to as *hyperfine splitting*. Basically it arises due to electron spin, and the Dirac theory was quite successful in explaining hyperfine splitting.

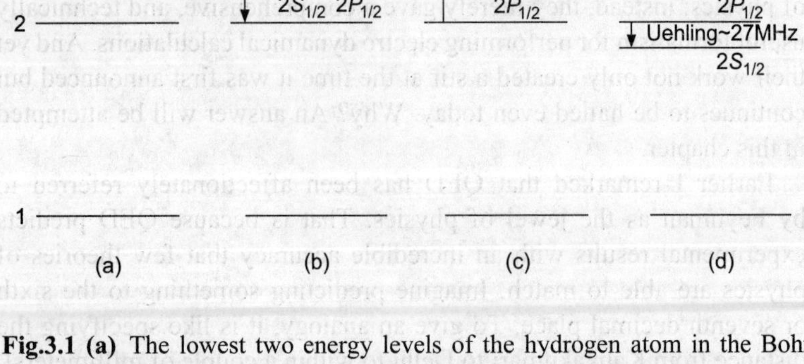

Fig.3.1 (a) The lowest two energy levels of the hydrogen atom in the Bohr model, (b) The same levels according to the (one-electron) Dirac theory. The $2P_{3/2} - 2P_{1/2}$ gap is due to hyperfine splitting, (c) Qualitative picture of Lamb shift, (d) Shift as determined by Uehling. *Caution*: Level schemes are schematic!

One prediction of Dirac's theory is that the $2S_{1/2}$ and $2P_{1/2}$ levels coincide. The spectrum in Fig. 3.1(b) does not show the effects of radiative corrections. One knows, however, that such corrections push the energy levels around, i.e., the level n is shifted from energy $E(n)$ to $E(n) + \Delta E(n)$ where $\Delta E(n)$ is the shift due to radiative correction. In this picture, one expects the following:

$$E(2S_{1/2}) \to E(2S_{1/2}) + \Delta E(2S_{1/2})$$

$$E(2P_{1/2}) \to E(2P_{1/2}) + \Delta E(2P_{1/2}).$$

There is no reason why $\Delta E(2S_{1/2})$ should equal $\Delta E(2P_{1/2})$. In that case, thanks to radiative corrections, a gap would now occur between the $2S_{1/2}$ and $2P_{1/2}$ levels as sketched in Fig. 3.1(c). This gap is called the Lamb shift. It is not expected according to the "simple one-electron" version of the Dirac theory, and indeed people at first believed that the $2S_{1/2}$ and $2P_{1/2}$ levels would be degenerate. Then came the negative-energy states, virtual processes and all that, and people realised that every level would get an energy shift of ΔE. In fact, Oppenheimer made an estimate of ΔE and was startled to obtain the answer ∞ ! Of course, it was realised that this result was not OK.

Soon everyone believed that radiative corrections existed and that they would contribute *finite* level shifts $\Delta E(n)$. The problem was, how to calculate them?

In 1936, Uehling made such an attempt and his thinking can be roughly understood as follows. Both the proton and the electron in the hydrogen atom are embedded in the vacuum. The vacuum charge therefore gets redistributed as sketched in Fig. 2.16. The net result of this vacuum polarisation is that the electrostatic interaction between the electron and the proton is changed from $(-e^2/r)$ to $(-e^2/r\varepsilon)$, where ε is the dielectric constant of the vacuum—in other words, there are non-Coulombic corrections. This of course is putting things rather naively but is nevertheless the gist of the whole business. Proceeding in this manner, Uehling found that the $2S_{1/2}$ and $2P_{1/2}$ levels move apart as in Fig. 3.1(d) by about 27 MHz.

A remark: In atomic physics, energy separations are often quoted in electron volts (eV). Historically, spectroscopists used frequency (ν) for this purpose. At times they quoted wave numbers ($= \nu/c = 1/\lambda$, the number of waves in 1 cm). The splitting computed by Uehling is in the radio frequency range.

Even prior to Uehling's estimate, there was some suspicion (based on inconclusive and poor resolution experiments) that the $2S_{1/2}$ and $2P_{1/2}$ levels were not coinciding but no one knew precisely what their separation was. It was only after the war that Lamb measured this shift and found it to be ~ 1000 MHz. We shall come to Lamb's experiment presently. What we note here is that Uehling's estimate was (i) quite small in magnitude (compared to the actual splitting that is), and (ii) of the wrong sign, i.e., the $2S$ level is depressed below the $2P$ level instead of being raised. This is not to say that vacuum polarisation effects are not relevant; just that there are other contributions as well, and which are more dominant.

Time now to say something about the original Lamb shift experiment which was performed in 1947 by Willis Lamb Jr. and Retherford. The history of this crucial experiment is given in Chapter 6. First let us consider the hydrogen spectrum again, in the region of interest. In Fig. 3.2(a) and (b) we see the situation without and with the Lamb shift. Without Lamb shift, the hyperfine splitting is around 11,000 MHz but on account of the Lamb shift, the $2P_{3/2} - 2S_{1/2}$ separation decreases to ~ 10,000 MHz. Lamb and Retherford essentially measured this transition frequency. For practical and technical reasons, they first applied a magnetic field before causing transitions. As a result of this field, $2P_{3/2}$ and $2S_{1/2}$ levels split as shown in Fig. 3.2(c).

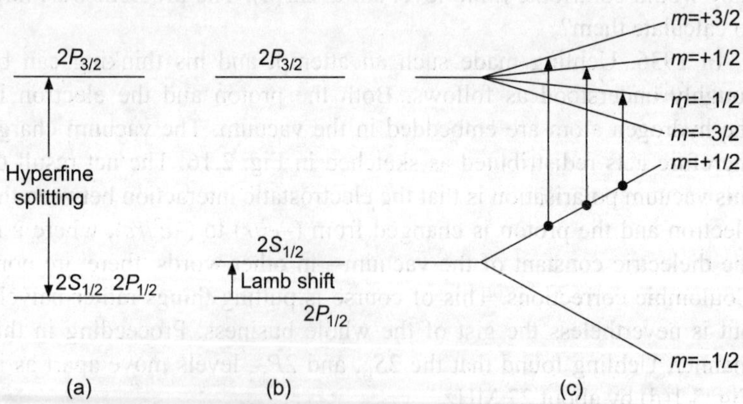

Fig.3.2 Once again the levels of H associated with principal quantum number equal to 2. (a) without Lamb shift, (b) with Lamb shift and (c) in the presence of a magnetic field. Some of the possible transitions from the (metastable) $2S_{1/2}$ sublevels to the (unstable) $2P_{3/2}$ sublevels are also shown.

Considering the $2S_{1/2}(m=+1/2)$ sublevel, four transitions are possible to the sublevels of the $2P_{3/2}$ level. Lamb and Retherford were able to observe three of these transitions.

Figure 3.3(a) shows the principle of their experiment. A beam of atomic hydrogen is produced by a furnace. Normally hydrogen is a molecule but in the furnace the molecules are dissociated into atoms. When the atomic beam emerges from the furnace, it encounters an electron beam. Due to electron bombardment, some of the atoms become excited. About 1 in 10^8 are in the excited metastable $2S$ state. When the atoms reach the detector they encounter a metal plate. The metastable atoms are able to cause electrons to be ejected from the metal plate and this produces a current. Therefore their presence can be detected. The atoms in the ground state, though numerous, go undetected because they do not eject electrons; they therefore cause no problem. If on the journey to the detector, the atoms in the $2S$ state are perturbed and made to go over to the $2P$ state, then from the latter they very quickly jump to the ground state. So by the time they reach the detector, they are no longer in the metastable state. Of course, once the atom reaches the ground state, the current detector is no longer sensitive to it.

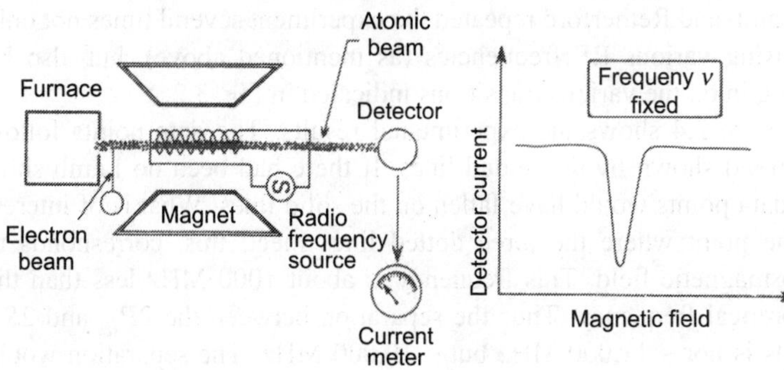

Fig.3.3 (a) shows the schematic of the arrangement used by Lamb and Retherford. An atomic beam of hydrogen is produced by a furnace. This beam is then bombarded by an electron beam causing some atoms to go into the metastable state. One atom in 10^8 is in the metastable $2S$ state. Only these atoms produce a current in the detector. En route to the detector, the beam passses through a magnetic field which splits the levels as in Fig. 3.2(c). If the beam is irradiated with a radio wave of the correct frequency, a transition to one of the $2P$ sublevels can be induced. The current then dips as in (b).

Lamb and Retherford skilfully exploited this fact. They made the atomic beam to pass through a radio frequency field which acts as a perturbation. A magnetic field is also applied splitting the atomic levels into their magnetic sublevels. The perturbation is most effective when the applied radio frequency (RF) precisely matches the separation between the $2S_{1/2}$ sublevels and the $2P_{3/2}$ sublevels. Remember, for a given value of the applied magnetic field, there is a unique separation between the sublevels.

The experiment is thus performed as follows: Produce the atomic beam. Then switch on the RF oscillator. The oscillator is capable of many different frequencies but in a given run, the frequency is kept fixed. The magnetic field is now switched on, and the field strength is gradually increased. During all this process, the detector current is constantly monitored. If a graph of the current versus the field is plotted, a dip would be found as in Fig. 3.3(b). The dip occurs because for that value of the magnetic field, the separation between the $2S$ and $2P$ sublevels matches the RF frequency. As a result, the metastable atoms get tipped from the $2S$ to the $2P$ level from where they instantly crash to the ground level. Thus fewer metastable atoms reach the detector, and the current is reduced.

Lamb and Retherford repeated the experiment several times not only by using various RF frequencies (as mentioned above), but also by tuning in on the various transitions indicated in Fig. 3.2.

Figure 3.4 shows the experimental results. The data points follow the trend shown by the dotted lines. If there had been no Lamb shift, the data points would have fallen on the solid lines. What is of interest is the point where the three dotted lines meet; this, corresponds to zero magnetic field. This frequency is about 1000 MHz less than the theoretical frequency. Thus the separation between the $2P_{3/2}$ and $2S_{1/2}$ levels is not ~ 11,000 MHz but ~ 10,000 MHz. The separation would have been 11,000 MHz if the $2S_{1/2}$ and $2P_{1/2}$ levels had coincided, as predicted by the Dirac one-electron theory—see Fig. 3.1(b). Since the separation is 10,000 MHz, Lamb and Retherford concluded that the $2S_{1/2}$ level is raised by ~ 1000 MHz with respect to the $2P_{1/2}$ level—see Fig. 3.1(c). This is the Lamb shift.

The experiment has been repeated subsequently by other workers, and more accurate values obtained for the Lamb shift.

The experiment of Lamb and Retherford clearly showed for the first time that the $2S$ and $2P$ levels are not coincident but are separated. It was then realised that this separation is entirely due to radiative

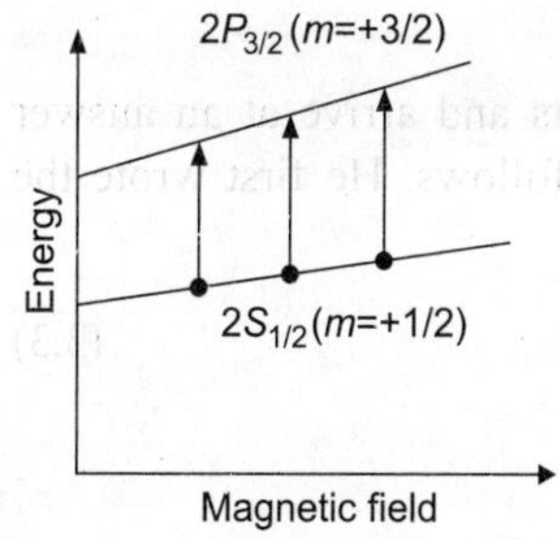

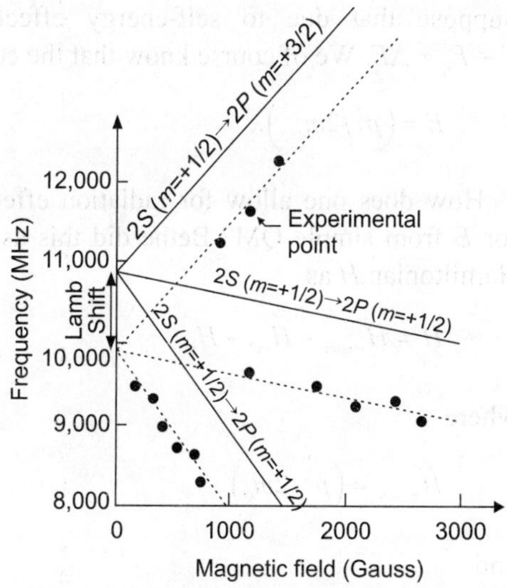

Fig.3.4 (a) shows the levels $2P_{3/2}(m = +3/2)$ and $2S_{1/2}(m = +1/2)$ as a function of the magnetic field. The frequency required to cause a transition between the two depends on the applied field, (b) is a summary of the results obtained by Lamb and Retherford. Each data point is obtained by holding the frequency at a particular value and sweeping the magnetic field to record a dip (as in Fig. 3.3(b)). The convergence point of the experimental lines (dotted curves) is different from that of the theoretical curves on account of the Lamb shift.

corrections, arising principally from self-energy effects and to a lesser extent from vacuum polarisation.

The time is now ripe to explain how the self-energy business, mentioned several times earlier, works in practice, and how it contributes to the Lamb shift. The best way of doing this is to start with a pioneering calculation of Bethe. As you will learn in Chapter 6, this was the first ray of sunshine emerging from behind the dark clouds. And yet, as you will presently see, Bethe's approach was simplicity itself.

Let us start with a single "free" electron. We wish to see how electromagnetic interaction would alter its energy. If m_0 is its mass and p the momentum, in simple-minded non-relativistic theory we would write its (kinetic) energy as

$$E_0 = \left(p^2/2m_0\right). \tag{3.1}$$

Suppose that due to self-energy effects the energy changes to $E = E_0 + \Delta E$. We of course know that the correct answer is

$$E = \left(p^2/2m_{\text{exp}}\right). \tag{3.2}$$

How does one allow for radiation effects and arrive at an answer for E from simple QM? Bethe did this as follows. He first wrote the Hamiltonian H as

$$H = H_{\text{matter}} + H_{\text{rad}} + H_{\text{int}} \tag{3.3}$$

where

$$H_{\text{matter}} = \left(\hat{p}^2/2m_0\right) \tag{3.4}$$

and

$$H_{\text{int}} = -\left(\frac{e}{m_0 c}\right)\hat{\mathrm{p}}.\hat{\mathrm{A}}. \tag{3.5}$$

I shall not write the expression for H_{rad} because I have already discussed it in Chapter 1; anyway, it is not very important for us right now. Treating H_{int} as a perturbation and going up to second order Bethe found (using free electron wave functions),

$$E = E_0 + \Delta E = \frac{p^2}{2m_0} - \frac{p^2}{2m_0}.\frac{\Delta m}{m_0}. \tag{3.6}$$

This result is easy to digest and obtain. We simply expand

$$\frac{p^2}{2\left(m_0 + \Delta m\right)},$$

assuming ($\Delta m/m_0$) is small. Remembering (3.2), this essentially means that

$$m_{\text{exp}} = m_0 + \Delta m, \tag{3.7}$$

i.e., that radiative correction acts as if the mass is increased by an amount Δm. Bethe obtained an expression for Δm in terms of free electron wave functions. This expression diverged but Bethe was not worried. Remember, so far we have considered an isolated electron.

Now the Lamb shift is not concerned with a *free* electron but an electron *bound* in the hydrogen atom. In other words, we need ΔE for the electron in hydrogen. Bethe calculates this more or less by the same procedure but with slight differences. Firstly he includes the electron – proton potential $V(r)$. Secondly he rewrites the Hamiltonian in terms of the observed mass $m_{exp} = (m_0 + \Delta m)$ of the electron, rather than in terms of m_0 as in (3.4) and (3.5). Thus, H_{rad} remains essentially the same as before but H_{matter} becomes

$$H_{matter} = \frac{\hat{p}^2}{2\left(m_{exp} - \Delta m\right)} + V(r) \tag{3.8}$$

while H_{int} becomes

$$H_{int} = -\frac{e}{\left(m_{exp} - \Delta m\right)c} . \hat{\text{p}} . \hat{\text{A}}. \tag{3.9}$$

Resorting to approximation,

$$H \sim H_{rad} + \frac{\hat{p}^2}{2m_{exp}} + V(r) - \underbrace{\frac{e^2}{m_{exp}c} . \hat{\text{p}} . \hat{\text{A}} + \frac{\Delta m}{m_{exp}} . \frac{p^2}{2m_{exp}}}_{\text{perturbation}} . \tag{3.10}$$

In the above, the perturbation term is explicitly identified. This calculation would give the energy level of the atom with radiation effects included. The calculations are made using hydrogen – atom wave functions. Bethe now calculates ΔE from the above by subtracting the result for E in (3.6). Notice that by subtracting the result for the isolated electron from that for the electron in the atom, Bethe is essentially subtracting one infinity from another to get a finite result. This trick is at times referred to as subtraction physics!

All that now remained was to use this technology to calculate the level shifts for the $2S$ and the $2P$ levels, i.e., $\Delta E\ (2S)$ and $\Delta E\ (2P)$. Bethe noted that the $2P$ level is hardly shifted whereas the $2S$ level shifts by

$$\frac{1}{3\pi}\frac{e^2}{\hbar c}\text{Ryd}\log\frac{K}{\langle E(2S)\rangle}. \tag{3.11}$$

Here Ryd is the Rydberg constant defined by

$$\text{Ryd} = \left(m_{exp}\,\alpha^2/2\right),\ \alpha = \left(e^2/\hbar c\right) = \text{Fine structure constant.}$$

$\langle E(2S)\rangle$ is the average excitation energy for the $2S$ state and K is a quantity related to the virtual photons participating in the self-energy business. Strictly speaking K must $\to \infty$ but using physical arguments Bethe set $K = m_{\text{exp}}c^2$. Plugging numbers into (3.7), Bethe obtained

Lamb shift ~ 1040 MHz,

quite close to the then measured value of ~ 1000 MHz. This was a welcome breakthrough for it revealed that the Lamb shift is caused essentially by self-energy effects. As Bethe wrote then, "the level shift due to interaction with radiation is a real effect and is of finite magnitude." At the same time, everyone, Bethe included, realised that this "back-of-the-envelope" estimate must be confirmed by proper, relativistic calculations, which of course was duly done. We shall now try to understand this in terms of Feynman diagrams.

The diagrams relevant are shown in Fig. 3.5. That in (a) is what we would consider in lowest-order, i.e., when we are not worried about radiative corrections. The simplest diagrams associated with radiative corrections are given in (b), (c), (d) and (e). Of these, c(i) and d(i) represent self-energy contributions. You would also notice a new type of diagram in c(ii) and d(ii). These are symbolic representations of the contributions from the counter-term. Among the remaining,

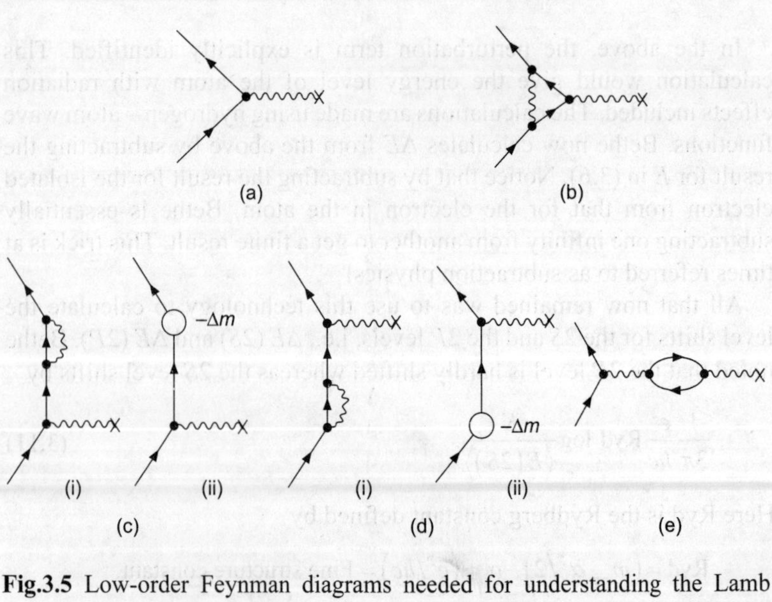

Fig.3.5 Low-order Feynman diagrams needed for understanding the Lamb shift. Of these, c(i) and d(i) describe self-energy effects while (e) pertains to vacuum polarisation. c(ii) and d(ii) are the diagrams for counter-term contributions.

(b) is associated with the anomalous magnetic moment of the electron (section 3.3) while (e) is associated with vacuum polarisation. If the famous Feynman tool kit is used and all the contributions are properly computed and added together, one obtains:

$$\text{Lamb shift} = \frac{4}{3\pi}.\alpha^5 m_{\exp} c^2 \log \frac{K}{\langle E(2S)\rangle} + \frac{11}{24} + \frac{1}{8} - \frac{1}{5}. \tag{3.12}$$

Here the first term is the Bethe contribution already familiar to us. The second term (11/24) arises due to a more delicate consideration of self-energy effects (i.e., diagrams (c) and (d)), and the last term (–1/5) is due to vacuum polarisation (i.e., diagram (e)); it is nothing but the Uehling contribution. This leaves the (1/8) term which Schwinger first drew attention to; it is due to magnetic effects (i.e., diagram (b)). Historically, both Feynman and Schwinger made a mistake in computing the (11/24) term! But they quickly rectified the error. The result in (3.12) is a first-cut answer from QED. It can be and has been refined to take into account (i) the shift of the 2*P* level and (ii) the contributions from the higher order diagrams.

A recent measurement of the Lamb shift gives a value of 1057.862 ± 0.020 MHz whereas QED (taking into account refinements mentioned above) predicts 1057.864 ± 0.014 MHz.

Lamb shift has also been measured in what is called muonic helium. Now the normal helium atom consists of an alpha particle core (i.e., two protons and two neutrons) and two electrons outside this core or nucleus. Suppose the electrons are stripped and replaced by a μ-meson which is a particle rather like the electron but much heavier. One then gets muonic helium. In this case, vacuum polarisation contributes 90% of the Lamb shift in contrast to the hydrogen atom where the contribution from vacuum polarisation is only ~ 10 %.

Once again let us understand the meaning of the Lamb shift. Essentially, it is the shift in the energy level of the electron due to radiative corrections. Seen this way, the difference in the energies given by (3.2) and (3.1) represents the radiative correction for a free electron. This, however, is not observable. By contrast, the Lamb shift in hydrogen is because the electron in hydrogen is a bound electron. We deal with this problem by *starting* from (3.2) and then of course doing an appropriate subtraction. To put it differently, Bethe in his pioneering calculation simply worked out the difference between the self-energy of a free electron and the self-energy of an electron in the hydrogen atom. There is an infinity implied in each of the two self-energies but they cancel each other—recall Fig. 2.14.

3.3 Anomalous magnetic moment

Another piece of experimental evidence that lends support to QED is the so-called anomalous magnetic moment of the electron. According to the Dirac theory, the electron behaves as if it has a magnetic moment $\mu = (e\hbar/2m_{exp}c)$. In CGS units, the value of the electron magnetic moment is -0.927×10^{-20} erg/gauss and is taken as 1 Bohr magneton. The measured value of the electron magnetic moment is slightly greater than 1 Bohr magneton, and the excess is called the anomalous contribution to the magnetic moment. Physically it arises due to the diagrams in Fig. 3.6, i.e., due to vacuum polarisation. If the external source corresponds to a uniform magnetic field, the process of Fig. 3.6 essentially endows the electron with an extra magnetic moment of $(\mu\alpha / 2\pi)$ where α is the fine structure constant. Thus, to lowest-order, the electron magnetic moment is not μ but

$$\mu\left(1+\frac{\alpha}{2\pi}\right) \sim 1.001162 \text{ Bohr magnetons.}$$

Early experiments showed that the magnetic moment was indeed slightly in excess of 1 Bohr magneton as expected according to the above estimate. Since then much progress has been made and more stringent tests applied. Upto third-order, one finds

$$\mu\left\{1+\frac{\alpha}{2\pi}-0.328,478,445\frac{\alpha^2}{\pi}+1.18311\frac{\alpha^3}{\pi}\right\}$$

$$= 1.001,159,652,359\,(282) \text{ Bohr magnetons}$$

The numbers in parenthesis denote uncertainties. By the way, to arrive at this number, as many as 891 Feynman diagrams had to be considered. Compare the above theoretical value with the experimental result.

1.001,159,652,410 (200) Bohr magneton

Just look at the match! No wonder QED is applauded so much.

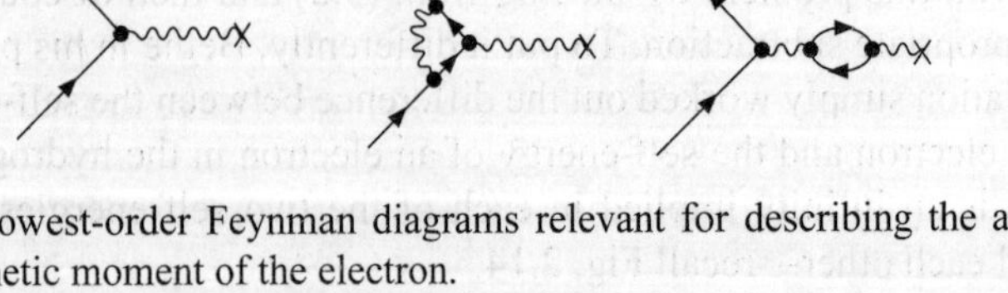

Fig.3.6 Lowest-order Feynman diagrams relevant for describing the anomalous magnetic moment of the electron.

3.4 Ground state separation in positronium

Just one more example of the early success scored by QED, and that relates to the splitting of the ground state of positronium. First I should explain what is meant by positronium. It is an imitation of the hydrogen atom in which the proton is replaced by a positron. Believe it or not, positronium is possible, has been produced in the lab and experimented upon. Of course with the positron and the electron so close to each other, one does not expect the positronium atom to live long and indeed it disappears or decays after a while, naturally into photons. But while it lives, the positronium atom has an energy level spectrum very much like the hydrogen atom has. We shall focus on the ground state 1*S*.

Now both the electron and the positron have spin 1/2. The two spins could combine to produce a total spin $J = 1$ or $J = 0$. As a result, the ground state splits into two states called triplet and singlet denoted by 1^3S and 1^1S respectively. We shall drop the principal quantum number and write these simply as ^3S and ^1S. Sometimes, positronium in these two states is referred to as ortho- and para-positronium respectively. Figure 3.7 shows the energy levels of these

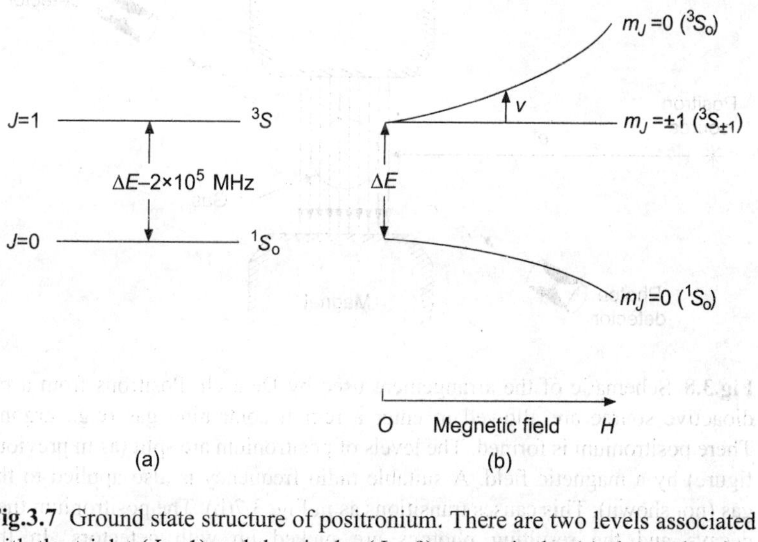

Fig.3.7 Ground state structure of positronium. There are two levels associated with the triplet ($J = 1$) and the singlet ($J = 0$) respectively, (a) shows the situation in zero magnetic field while (b) shows how the levels split in the field. Deutsch produced transitions from the $m_J = \pm 1$ levels to $m_J = 0$ level as shown by the arrow. From this he inferred ΔE. The value so obtained is different from the predictions of the Dirac theory. The difference is due to radiative corrections.

two states in the presence of a magnetic field. Observe that even at zero field, there is a frequency separation of about 200,000 MHz between the triplet and the singlet states. This is hyperfine splitting in positronium—see Fig. 3.7. Dirac's theory predicts a hyperfine splitting ΔE, but the value of ΔE is modified by radiative corrections.

As mentioned earlier, positronium is unstable and annihilates. Decay in the triplet state results in three photons (for reasons of conservation of momentum) while decay of the singlet state results in two photons flying away roughly 180° from each other. Comparatively speaking, the triplet state is longer lived, having a lifetime of ~ 1.4×10^{-7}s whereas the singlet state has a lifetime of only 1.25×10^{-10}s.

The small separation between the triplet and singlet states was measured for the first time by Martin Deutsch by a clever technique. The idea can be appreciated by considering Fig. 3.8. Basically, one tips positronium in the $^3S_{\pm 1}$ state to $^3S_0$ state by applying a radio field of appropriate frequency. In the $^3S_{\pm 1}$ state the decay is slow but when pushed into the $^3S_0$ state, the decay is more rapid. This is because the $^3S_0$ state has strong overlap with the $^1S_0$ state.

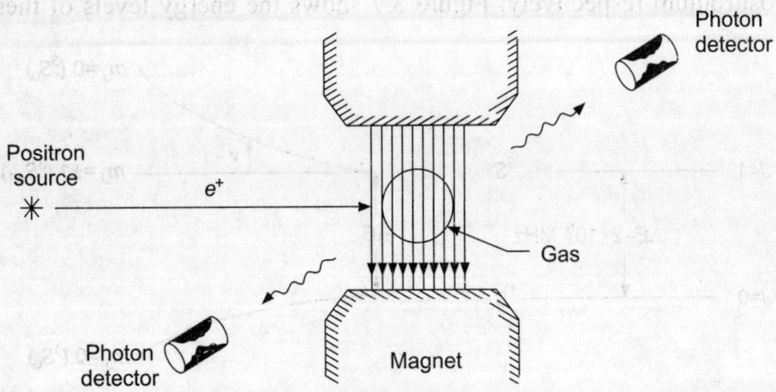

Fig.3.8 Schematic of the arrangement used by Deutsch. Positrons from a radioactive source are allowed to enter a region containing gas (e.g., argon). There positronium is formed. The levels of positronium are split (as in previous figure) by a magnetic field. A suitable radio frequency is also applied to the gas (not shown). This causes transitions as in Fig. 3.7(b). The positronium then decays and the resulting photons are picked up with detectors. In the experiment, the frequency v is fixed and the field H is varied to cause the transition.

Figure 3.9 shows a schematic of the result in a typical run. The resonance frequency (ν) measured depends on H the field applied and ΔE the singlet – triplet separation, i.e., the separation between ^3S and ^1S at zero field. Knowing ν and H, ΔE can be obtained. Deutsch measured a value of $(2.032 \pm 0.003) \times 10^5$ MHz for ΔE. Two recent values are:

2.033, 870(16) $\times 10^5$ MHz

2.033, 849(12) $\times 10^5$ MHz.

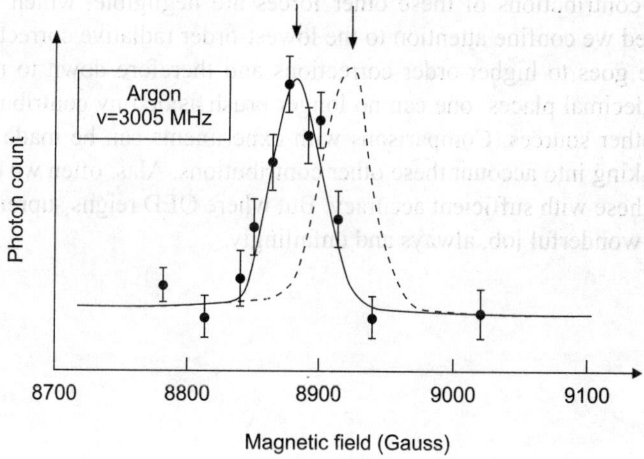

Fig.3.9 Typical data obtained by Deutsch. The dots show experimental points. Each dot represents the coincidence counts of the two detectors of the previous figure. The vertical lines indicate statistical errors. The frequency is kept fixed and H varied. At one value of the field, there is transition from $m_J = \pm 1$ to the $m_J = 0$ level (as shown in Fig. 3.7). The photon counts then increase. The solid line is a smooth curve drawn through the data points. The dotted line is the curve expected on the basis of the Dirac theory. The peak shift is due to radiative corrections.

The splitting ΔE with lowest-order radiative corrections included is given by

$$\Delta E = \frac{1}{2}\alpha^2 \text{ Ryd}\left\{\frac{7}{3} - \frac{32}{9} + 2\log 2\frac{\alpha}{\pi}\right\}.$$

ΔE calculated using this formula comes out to be 2.0337×10^5 MHz.

I have confined myself mainly to the earliest verifications of the radiative corrections predicted by QED. Needless to say that QED has been tested repeatedly on later occasions, even more stringently, and it has always come out with flying colours. One must also mention that when radiation corrections became small (as they do in higher- orders), one must start worrying about non-QED contributions to the physical process under consideration. We must never forget that besides the electromagnetic force there are other forces in Nature. They are always there in the background, e.g., the nuclear force. In our enthusiasm to check QED, we have ignored these other forces. This is OK as long as the contributions of these other forces are negligible, which is so provided we confine attention to the lowest-order radiative corrections. As one goes to higher-order corrections and therefore down to many many decimal places, one can no longer brush aside tiny contributions from other sources. Comparisons with experiments can be made only after taking into account these other contributions. Alas, often we don't know these with sufficient accuracy. But where QED reigns supreme, it does a wonderful job, always and unfailingly.

4 *Where's The Magic?*

> The preparation of finite physically meaningful results from a divergent theory is always a tricky business. It was very difficult in the mid-thirties. One reason was the ... absence of a suitable manifestly relativistically invariant theory ...
>
> *R. Jost*

4.1 Introduction

Notwithstanding my sales pitch for QED (especially in the last chapter, you must be quite perplexed. Behind all the razzle-dazzle about diagrams and what not, what really is happening? After all one is merely doing perturbation theory, in which case why was QED II such a disaster while QED III is a stunning success? This chapter is intended as a partial answer to this question—partial because a full answer requires one to go into elaborate technical details which are beyond our scope. But an overview covering the essentials is possible, which is what we shall attempt. (Even this may be a bit technical!)

4.2 Relativistic covariance

Forget QED for a moment and consider special relativity (see Box 4.1; for more details, see the companion Volume *At the Speed of Light*). There we are mainly concerned with the description of the same events in two inertial frames moving uniformly with respect to each other. Observers in the two frames can relate to each other via Lorentz transformations. If the theory (which describes the events) is properly constructed, certain quantities (e.g., charge) will remain invariant while going from one frame to another while certain equations (e.g., force equation) will retain their form, i.e., remain relativistically covariant.

Box 4.1 Here's a primer on special relativity as needed here. Figure (a) shows space-time (1 + 1). This is for illustration only; we should really consider 4-dimensional space-time (3 + 1). AB is the trajectory of a particle; it is usual to call it a world line. This is with respect to an observer in a particular inertial frame. *OL* is the world line for a photon emitted at the origin at the time $t = 0$. The region above the photon world line—also called *light cone*—is said to be *time-like*, and the region below *space-like*. Distances between events, e.g., A and B, are measured according to the rule $s^2 = c^2t^2 - x^2$. Clearly, the distance between two points on the light cone is always zero. In the time-like region, $s^2 > 0$ and in the space-like region, $s^2 < 0$.

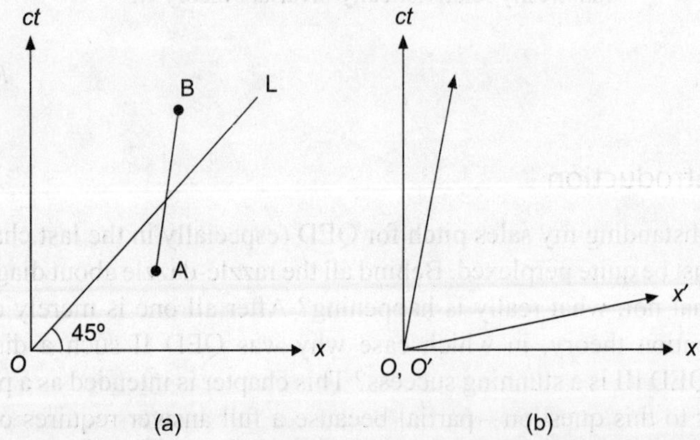

Suppose there are two observers who are riding inertial frames which move with a uniform velocity v with respect to each other. Let O be stationary and *O′* the observer in motion. The axes pertaining to the two would be as in figure (b). Transformations from one frame to another are via Lorentz transformations. Any physical theory must be consistent with these transformations. In turn, this implies that certain equations must preserve their form when going from one frame to another. When this happens, one says the equations are relativistically covariant. Maxwell's equations are relativistically covariant. Let $(E_x, E_y, E_z; B_x, B_y, B_z)$ be the field components in frame *O*. Via Lorentz transformations one can determine the components $(E'_x, E'_y, E'_z; B'_x, B'_y, B'_z)$ in frame *O′*. Let us now consider an example of form preservation. One of Maxwell's equations is

$$\frac{\partial E_z}{\partial y} - \frac{\partial E_y}{\partial z} = -\frac{\partial B_x}{\partial t} \qquad (1)$$

This is in the O frame. In the O' frame, the corresponding equation is,

$$\frac{\partial E'_z}{\partial y'} - \frac{\partial E'_y}{\partial z'} = -\frac{\partial B'_x}{\partial t'}. \tag{2}$$

Observe that (1) and (2) have the *same form*. This is characteristic of relativistic covariance. Using Lorentz transformations, one can arrive at (2) for (1) or vice versa.

With this preamble, we come now to the sensitive question of QED and relativistic covariance. Both in QED II and in QED III, electron propagation is described in terms of the Dirac equation. As you know, Dirac was led to this equation while searching for a wave equation that respected relativity. So both QED II and III are off to an auspicious start, so to speak. Why then does QED II fail whereas QED III is able to deliver the goods?

You might have heard the saying that justice must not only be done but must also *appear* to be done. The business of relativistic covariance in field theory is something like that. True both QED II and QED III start swearing by relativity but along the line, QED II goes astray! That's what leads to disaster. In QED III on the other hand, the requirements of relativity are respected in every stage of the perturbation calculation. As Oppenheimer puts it, "… not merely the field equations themselves but the whole method of approximation and solution *must at all stages preserve [relativistic] covariance*." Schwinger makes a similar remark: "A version of the theory was needed that *manifested covariance at every stage of the calculation*." I must hasten to add that covariance merely ensures logical consistency which of course is a must; infinities are *not* avoided. They have to be tackled differently, essentially via the renormalisation cum counter-term technique. This total package was proposed independently by Tomonaga, Schwinger and Feynman.

Notation: Normally while discussing space-time diagrams, we consider for convenience, 1-space plus 1-time. In reality we need to consider 4-dimensional space-time comprising three dimensions of space and one of time. Since space and time get mixed up, one finds it convenient to use a 4-vector notation. Thus (x, t) is written as a single 4-vector x with components (x_0, x_1, x_2, x_3). Of these, x_1, x_2, x_3 are the same as the components of the ordinary three-dimensional vector x. The remaining component x_0 is given by ct. Relativity thrives on 4-vectors. Thus (A, ψ) is compressed into a 4-vector A.

Consider a field $\psi(x)$. In QED, this could refer either to the electromagnetic field or the matter field. In the former case one must specify the commutator $[\psi(x), \psi(x')]$ and in the latter case the anti-commutator $\{\psi(x), \psi(x')\}$. I shall not tax you with all the details. This brings us to the basic question of formulating QM in a relativistically covariant way. In the beginning, people thought if one had a wave equation that respected relativity (the Klein-Gordon equation in the case of spin 0 particles and the Dirac equation in the case of spin 1/2 particles), then everything was OK thereafter. The disaster with infinities showed that this was not so. Painfully the realisation dawned that when we consider evolution in QM—be it the evolution of the wave function via the Schroedinger equation or the evolution of operators via the Heisenberg equation of motion—we must be careful about the requirements of relativity during the process of evolution also. This is the point we shall take up next.

4.3 Schwinger–Tomonaga equation

Consider the Schroedinger equation

$$i\hbar \frac{\partial \Psi(\mathrm{x},t)}{\partial t} = H\Psi(\mathrm{x},t) \tag{4.1}$$

This belongs to the pre-relativistic species of QM, and therefore time t plays the role of a mere parameter. Another way of saying this is that events are described with respect to one particular inertial or reference frame. In the present case this would not do. What we really need is an evolution equation somewhat like (4.1) but one which generalises it, i.e., is not tied to one frame of reference.

Before we consider generalisation, there is one important detail that must be attended to. In Part I, I told you something about how time evolution is usually studied in QM. There are two points of view, the Schroedinger representation in which the state vector Ψ is time dependent but operators are not, and the Heisenberg representation wherein operators are time dependent but the state vector is not. There is yet another representation called the *interaction* representation which is sort of between the two mentioned above. This is important for our present purposes.

Let the Hamiltonian H in (4.1) have the form $H = H_0 + H_I$ where H_0 is the unperturbed part and H_I is the perturbation. We now write

$$\Psi(t) = e^{iH_0 t/\hbar}\psi_s(t), \tag{4.2}$$

where $\psi_s(t)$ is the wave function in the Schroedinger representation.

With a bit of manipulation, it is then easy to show that

$$i\hbar\frac{\partial\Psi(t)}{\partial t}=H_I^{(IR)}(t)\Psi(t). \tag{4.3}$$

Here

$$H_I^{(IR)}(t)=e^{iH_0t/\hbar}H_Ie^{-iH_0t/\hbar}, \tag{4.4}$$

and is H_I in the new representation. I want you to focus on (4.3) because we are after something that looks rather like that equation.

We are now ready to consider the generalisation I mentioned earlier. As I already told you (4.1) pegs description to one particular inertial frame. In practical terms, we single out a special type of surface in space-time for which t = constant—see Fig. 4.1(a). This "flat" surface is space-like (recall Box 4.1). A more general version of a space-like surface σ which is not "flat" is shown in Fig. 4.1(b). How do we know if σ is space-like or not? Simple. Draw normals to σ as shown; if all the normals are time-like (recall Box 4.1), then σ is space-like even if it is not flat as in 4.1(a). Notice that since σ is not flat, time is not the same for two observers riding on the surface. This is an important generalisation.

The equation we are after is one which describes what happens to the state vector $\Psi(\sigma)$ when σ evolves as in Fig. 4.1(c). This equation was first discovered by Tomonaga and is given by

$$i\hbar c\frac{\delta\Psi(\sigma)}{\delta\sigma(x)}=H_I(x)\Psi(\sigma). \tag{4.5}$$

Several comments are needed. Firstly,

$$H_I(x)=e^{iH_0t/\hbar}H_I(\mathrm{x})e^{-iH_0t/\hbar}. \tag{4.6}$$

Secondly (4.5) is a functional *differential equation* but in spirit, it does essentially the same job as (4.3). I should add that (4.5) was independently discovered by Schwinger; it is therefore called the Schwinger-Tomonaga equation (or the other way about sometimes).

Recall that the usual wave function $\psi(\mathrm{x}, t)$ has a probabilistic interpretation. Tomonaga discovered that in relativistic field theory, it is not possible to give a physically meaningful probabilistic interpretation unless Ψ is defined via (4.5). In case you are uneasy about weird surfaces evolving in space-time, let me assure you that at the working level one is not confronted with such complications!

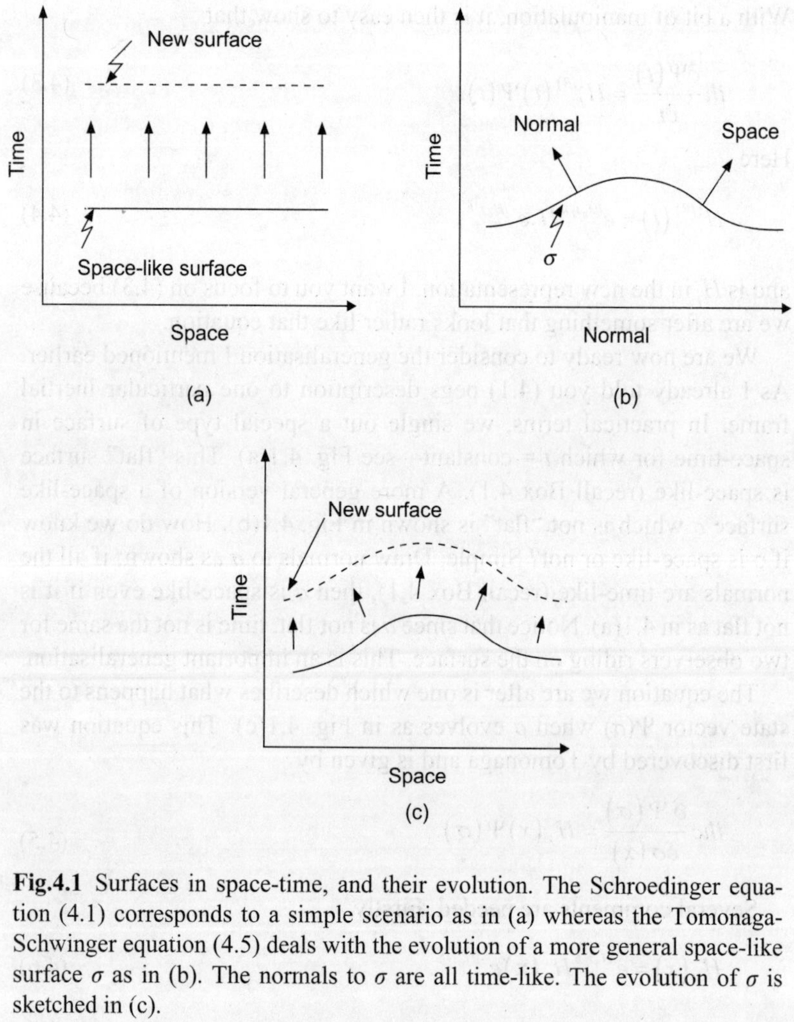

Fig.4.1 Surfaces in space-time, and their evolution. The Schroedinger equation (4.1) corresponds to a simple scenario as in (a) whereas the Tomonaga-Schwinger equation (4.5) deals with the evolution of a more general space-like surface σ as in (b). The normals to σ are all time-like. The evolution of σ is sketched in (c).

The ball game now becomes a bit clearer. The first order of business is to get at Ψ. And we want a Ψ that is not tied to any particular reference frame. So we enlarge our scope and widen our hunt for a $\Psi(\sigma)$ rather than settling for a mere $\Psi(x)$. With this, state vectors $\Psi(x)$ and $\Psi(x')$ can be linked, related and all that, provided of course $\Psi(x)$ and $\Psi(x')$ lie on σ which we assume to be the case. Things are now relativistically covariant, and there are no problems with the probabilistic interpretation.

Even this is not enough. We want to study how Ψ evolves under perturbation which then brings us to (4.5) where we find ourselves working in the interaction representation. How do we link (4.5) to doing perturbation theory to various orders? This is the question we shall address next.

4.4 Time evolution and the *S*-matrix

Let us simplify matters and consider time evolution rather than σ evolution. We ask: How does one relate $\Psi(t)$ to the wave function $\Psi(t_0)$ corresponding to an earlier time, i.e., $t > t_0$? All we have to do is to take (4.5) and integrate from t_0 to t. We then get

$$\Psi(t) = \Psi(t_0) - (i/\hbar)\int_{t_0}^{t}\Psi(t')H_I(t')\,dt'. \tag{4.7}$$

Even if you don't quite follow this, just take it as an equation that enables one to arrive at $\Psi(t)$ starting from $\Psi(t_0)$. In fact, the spirit of this equation is quite similar to that of (2.2) which we had earlier discussed. To make things more formal, we rewrite (4.7) as

$$\Psi(t) = U(t,t_0)\Psi(t_0) \tag{4.8}$$

where $U(t, t_0)$ is a unitary operator which acting on $\Psi(t_0)$ takes it to $\Psi(t)$. So it is rather like our old friend, the kernel K.

Instead of starting at time t_0, let us go far far back to $-\infty$ and from there march to the distant future, i.e., $+\infty$, via t_0 and then t. This sweeping evolution can be comprehensively written as

$$U(\infty,t)U(t,t_0)U(t_0,-\infty).$$

It is customary to compress this into $S(\infty, -\infty)$ or even denote it simply as S. This S is referred to as the *S-matrix*.

Historically, the S-matrix was introduced by Heisenberg way back in the mid-thirties. Heisenberg believed that the divergence difficulties of relativistic field theory could be avoided by the introduction of a new fundamental constant that has the dimensions of length. Heisenberg thought that this fundamental length would play a role similar to h. At present we know of no such constant but Heisenberg believed that it would be discovered one day, whereupon quantum mechanics would be suitably revised. And this new (yet-to-be-discovered) version of quantum theory would be rid of infinities. Heisenberg was also of the view that many quantities which we now treat as observables, would then lose that status. In preparation for such a future theory, he tried to describe physical processes without resorting to the Hamiltonian, and this is what led him to the *S*-matrix.

Getting back to (4.5), let us suppose that H_I was absent at $t = -\infty$, that it was then switched on and slowly allowed to grow to its full value. Let Φ be the "bare" state at start. Even as H_I builds up, Φ gets transformed to Ψ. Likewise let us also, suppose that eventually H_I is slowly turned off so that at $t = +\infty$, the system returns to a bare state. This ON-OFF scenario is schematically described in Fig. 4.2. From it, the following facts become evident:

1. $\Psi(t_0) = U(t_0, -\infty)\Phi$
2. $\Psi(t) = U(t, t_0)\Psi(t_0)$
3. $\Phi' = U(\infty, t)\Psi(t)$
4. $\Phi' = S\Phi = U(\infty, t)U(t, t_0)U(t_0, -\infty)\Phi$.

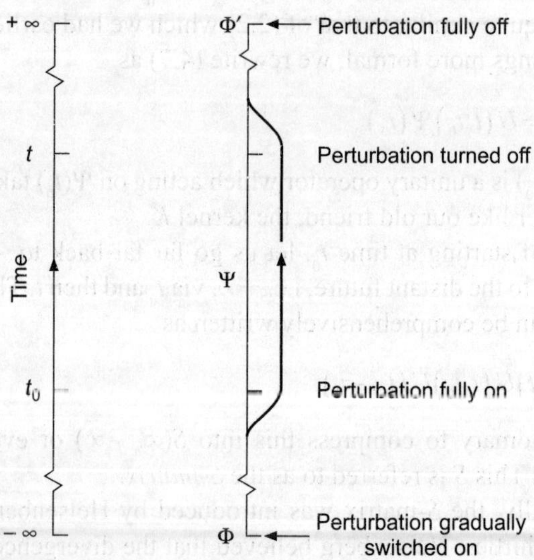

Fig.4.2 Schematic illustration of the evolution of state and the effect of perturbation. Here Φ is the state appropriate to H_0 and Ψ is the state in the presence of the perturbation H_I. The unitary matrix U that governs the entire process involves H_I as in (4.7). The perturbation is switched on and off slowly.

If we consider an isolated atom and regard H_I as the interaction between the electron and its own radiation field, then the perturbation is never really absent. Under the circumstances, our switching H_I on and then switching it off later is purely for operational convenience. In other words, a matrix element like $\langle \Psi' | R | \Psi \rangle$ can be manipulated into the form $\langle \Phi' | ...R... | \Phi \rangle$ and then evaluated.

4.5 The *U*-matrix and perturbation theory

We now consider $U(t, t_0)$ which carries $\Psi(t_0)$ to $\Psi(t)$. U is built up from the action of H_I which could repeatedly act during the period $(t - t_0)$.

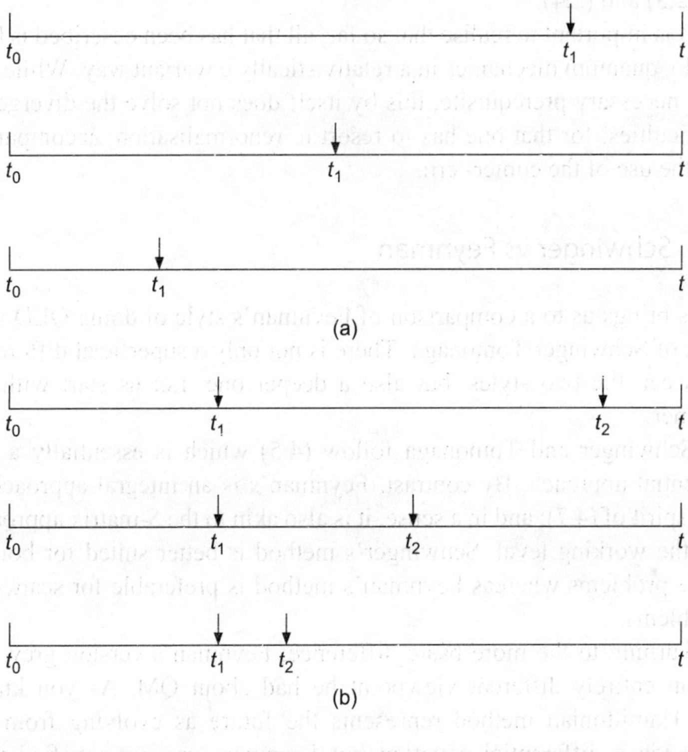

Fig.4.3 Illustrated here is the spirit of (4.9). (a) shows the perturbation acting in the first order. The instant of action t_1 could be anywhere between t_0 and t and some samples are shown; one must of course integrate over all possibilities. In the second-order (see b), for each t_1, t_2 could be anywhere between 0 and t_1, and t_1 itself could vary. To cover all possibilities obviously we must integrate over both t_2 and t_1. The nesting in higher-orders is similar.

Formally this is expressed by

$$U(t,t_0) = 1 + \left(\frac{-i}{\hbar}\right) \int_{t_0}^{t} dt_1 H_I(t_1) + \left(\frac{-i}{\hbar}\right)^2 \int_{t_0}^{t} dt_1 \int_{t_0}^{t_1} dt_2 H_I(t_1) H_I(t_2) + \ldots \tag{4.9}$$

The idea behind (4.9) is illustrated in Fig. 4.3.

Result (4.9) may now be used to compute the transition amplitude $\langle \Psi(t) | \Psi(t_0) \rangle$. We then effectively end up with the same expression as in (2.3) and (2.4).

It is important to realise that so far, all that has been described is how to do, quantum mechanics in a relativistically covariant way. While this is a necessary prerequisite, this by itself does not solve the divergence difficulties; for that one has to resort to renormalisation, accompanied by the use of the conter-term.

4.6 Schwinger vs Feynman

This brings us to a comparison of Feynman's style of doing QED with that of Schwinger/Tomonaga. There is not only a superficial difference between the two styles, but also a deeper one. Let us start with the former.

Schwinger and Tomonaga follow (4.5) which is essentially a differential approach. By contrast, Feynman's is an integral approach in the spirit of (4.7); and in a sense, it is also akin to the *S*-matrix approach. At the working level, Schwinger's method is better suited for bound-state problems whereas Feynman's method is preferable for scattering problems.

Turning to the more basic difference, Feynman's version grew out of an entirely different viewpoint he had about QM. As you know, the Hamiltonian method represents the future as evolving from the past via a differential equation but Feynman was not satisfied with that because he wanted to take in both the past and the future in one grand sweep. You might recall from Part I that Hamilton's equations of motion (the forerunner of Heisenberg's equations of motion) were deduced from an action principle. Action is more fundamental than the equations of motion themselves, the attractive thing about it being that it is relativistically invariant. No wonder Feynman was drawn to it (recall section 2.2 in Part I). As he observes:

> The Hamiltonian form of the equations develops the future from the instantaneous present. But for different observers in relative motion the instantaneous present is different, and corresponds to a different 3-dimensional cutoff space-time. Thus the temporal analysis of different observers is different and their Hamiltonian equations are developing the process in different ways. These differences are irrelevant, however, for the solution is the same in any space-time frame. By forsaking the Hamiltonian method, the wedding of relativity and quantum mechanics can be accomplished most naturally.

4.7 The Path-integral method

Let us look at this business in slightly greater detail, starting with some introductory remarks by Feynman himself:

> It is a curious historical fact that modern quantum mechanics began with two quite different mathematical formulations: the differential equation of Schroedinger, and the matrix algebra of Heisenberg. The two, apparently dissimilar approaches, were proved to be mathematically equivalent. These two points of view were destined to complement one another and to be ultimately synthesized in Dirac's transformation theory.

Feynman proposes a third approach in which a probability amplitude is associated with an entire motion of a particle as a function of time, i.e., *an entire evolution from an initial to a final state*, rather than simply with a position of a particle at a particular time. Commending it, Feynman observes:

> This formulation is mathematically equivalent to the more usual formulations. There are, therefore, no fundamentally new results. However, there is a pleasure in recognising old things from a new point of view. Also, there are problems for which the new point of view offers a distinct advantage.

Not surprisingly, this method of doing QM has come to be known as the *path-integral method.* Let us try to understand what exactly this new point of view means, and then how it confers advantages. Consider Fig. 4.4 which shows space-time (1 + 1). Shown here is a particle trajectory (or world line if you prefer). The trajectory happens to lie in a region *R*. Based on intuitive reasoning, Feynman makes the following postulate:

> Suppose an ideal measurement (whatever that means!) is performed to determine whether the trajectory lies in *R* or not. The probability that the result would be yes is equal to the absolute square of a sum of complex, amplitudes, one associated with each possible path in *R*.

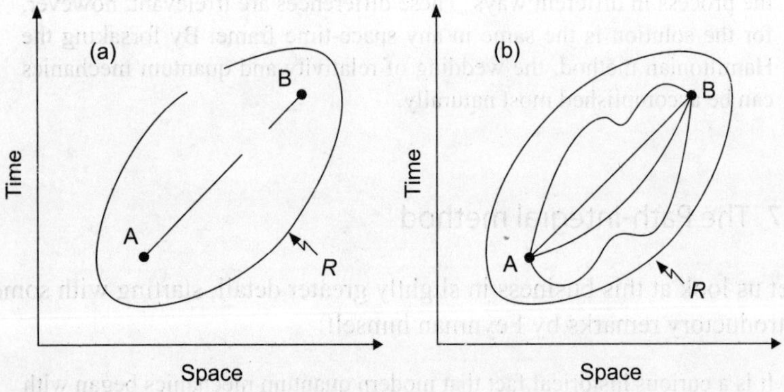

Fig.4.4(a) Shows a certain region *R* and a path or a world line contained in that. In QM, the progress of a particle from A to B is described by an amplitude and a phase; the tatter is related to the action *S*. To obtain the probability for the path to be in *R*, one must integrate over all paths—see(b).

This requires some explanation. In Fig.4.4(b) are shown many paths, all lying within *R*. Let $\psi_1, \psi_2 \ldots$ denote the "complex contributions" from these different paths. What Feynman's postulate says is: Probability of path lying in $R = \left|\sum_i \psi_i\right|^2$ where $\sum_i$ is a sum that runs over all paths in *R*. This brings us to Feynman's second postulate which is:

> The magnitudes of the ψ's are the same, i.e., $|\psi_1| = |\psi_2| = |\psi_3| = \ldots$ but the phases vary. In fact, the phase of ψ_i is the classical action (in units of $\hbar$) of the path *i*, i.e., phase of $\psi_i = e^{i S/\hbar}$ where
>
> $$S = \int_A^B L dt$$
>
> is the classical action. (Recall equation (2.1) in Part I.)

Two important points must be noted at this stage. First is that whereas in classical mechanics the particle would choose that particular path for which the action S is an extremum (recall Chapter 2, Part I), in quantum mechanics *all* paths between A and B (in Fig.4.4) must be considered. Secondly, paths are possible in which the particle travels backward in time. Since one wants to allow for this possibility, one does not want to be restricted by a formalism which allows time evolution only from the past to the future namely, the Hamiltonian formalism. I suppose you can now appreciate why Feynman wants to treat the past and the future in a symmetric fashion. In fact there is more to it as I shall point out shortly.

There is yet another reason why Feynman wants this action-based formulation of QM. He says, "if two systems A and B interact, the coordinates of one of the systems, say B, may be eliminated from the equations describing the motion of A." This statement might appear vague but becomes meaningful if we consider Fig. 2.13. We have here an "isolated" electron going say from x_A to x_B. Of course, during the journey the electron can emit and absorb photons. Naturally these virtual photons would affect the electron—this we already know. Feynman would like to describe the motion of the electron, eliminating all the (virtual) photon coordinates and incorporating their effects in the electron itself; the path-integral form of doing QM allows him to do so.

4.8 Elimination of photons

Why is Feynman so anxious to get rid of these (virtual) photons in the final description? The answer becomes clearer if for a minute we consider standard classical electrodynamics. One first splits the electromagnetic field into a longitudinal part and a transverse part. Both parts are then described in terms of oscillators. However, electromagnetic radiation is described purely by transverse waves which means the transverse oscillators alone must be retained and the longitudinal oscillators got rid of. One knows how to do this. But there is a problem. We can talk of longitudinal and transverse only with reference to a particular frame. As a result, what is pure longitudinal for one observer may only be partially so for another. In other words, this elimination business is not relativistically invariant. If now all the oscillators can be eliminated at one stroke, then there is no problem with relativistic invariance; nor is there any problem with gauge invariance.

There is deeper significance to this business of getting rid of virtual photons. One can understand it a bit better by considering the interaction between two electrons. One can say electron 1 produces a field which then interacts with electron 2. If one thinks of the field in quantum language, one would say that electron 1 emits a photon which is absorbed by the second electron. (Obviously, the photon is virtual.) If photons are dispensed with, it means that fields are abolished.

How is interaction possible without fields? The clue is provided by Newton's theory of gravitation. Newton's law of gravitation simply says that one mass attracts another; it does not demand a field. Well, suppose there are two masses m_1 and m_2. If we move m1, it alters the force on m_2. How does m_2 know m1 is moving? Newton explained it away as "action at a distance". He did not bring in any gravitational field (that came later with general relativity). In the present case, by "abolishing" the electromagnetic field, one is sort of going back to the action-at-a-distance picture for electromagnetic interactions.

Don't get shocked, for this is all a way of doing things. As Feynman himself says:

> Electrodynamics can be looked upon in two equivalent and complementary ways. One is as the description of the behaviour of the field (Maxwell's equations). The other is as a direct interaction at a distance (albeit delayed in time) between the charges … Roughly, the field point of view is most practical for problems involving real quanta, while the interaction view is best for the discussion of virtual quanta.

4.9 A fudge and a new cutoff

Path integrals, getting rid of oscillators and all that is fine but they alone are not sufficient for tackling the infinities. Some extra magic is needed, and let us now see how Feynman performs it.

We focus on the self-energy problem: There is an isolated electron, and during its jaunt it keeps emitting and absorbing photons rather like a chap tossing and catching a ball while walking. We know how to draw diagrams for this process—we did it in Fig.2.13. Calculating the self-energy means calculating the contributions from all these diagrams and adding them together. There is trouble even with the simplest of these diagrams, i.e., Fig. 2.13(b) as it gives a contribution of infinity. Experts have analysed why this infinity crops up. Suppose one goes into the momentum representation. As I told you earlier, one must then specify the momentum $\hbar k$ of the virtual photon. This k can be anything from 0 to ∞. So one must integrate over k but the integration proves nasty. Therefore one does not go all the way to but cuts off at some value, k_c say. This leads to the result (first obtained by Weisskopf) that

$$\Delta E \sim \log\left(\frac{\hbar k_c}{m_0 c}\right). \tag{4.10}$$

When $k_c \to \infty$, ΔE diverges logarithmically. The problem thus is in taking proper account of the contributions of photons of all k.

Feynman discovered a way of taking account of all photons which gave a *finite* answer. But this called for, as he puts it, changing the rules of the game somewhat. Consider two electrons distance x apart. If the first electron emits a photon, the latter would reach the second electron at time $t = x/c$. Recall now how "distance" s is defined in space-time (see Box 4.1). In this case $s^2 = c^2t^2 - x^2 = 0$. In other words, according to standard wisdom, interaction between the two electrons is possible only when $s^2 > 0$. Feynman decides to relax this rule and permit interaction between charges even for $s^2 \neq 0$. However, this concession is mild and restricted to only small positive values of s^2. The meaning of this rather vague statement is made a bit more precise in Figs.4.5 and 4.6. Notice the two curves in Fig. 4.6,

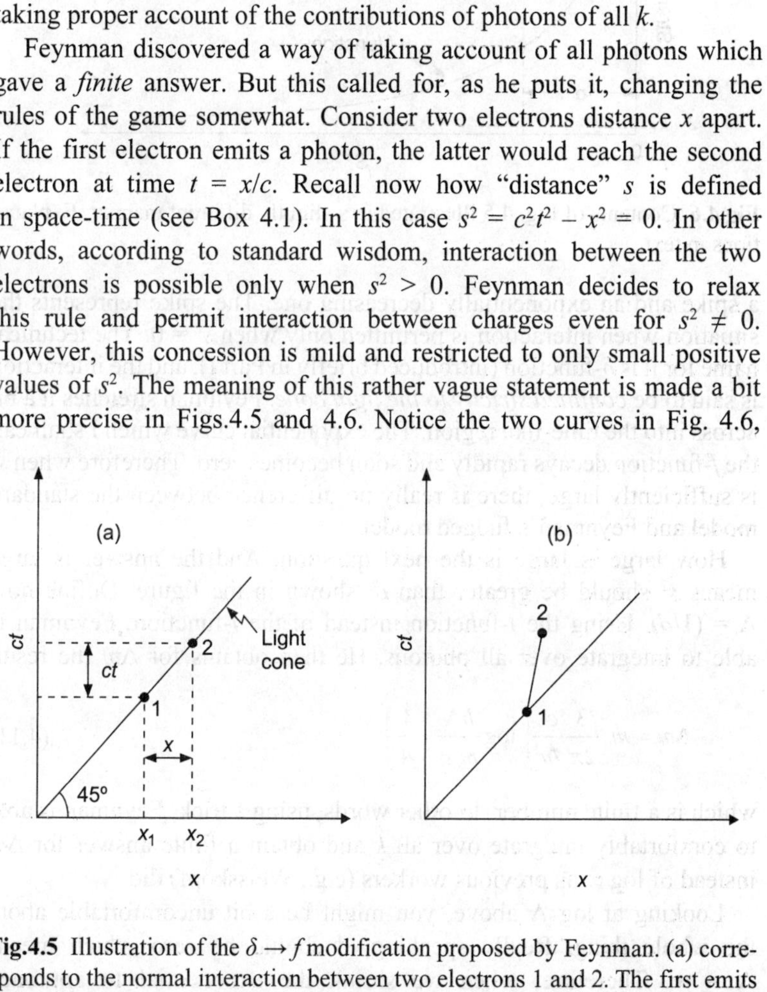

Fig.4.5 Illustration of the $\delta \to f$ modification proposed by Feynman. (a) corresponds to the normal interaction between two electrons 1 and 2. The first emits an electromagnetic wave which reaches 2 at time $t = (x/c)$ later. Correspondingly, $s = 0$. Feynman relaxes this law to permit interactions as in (b).

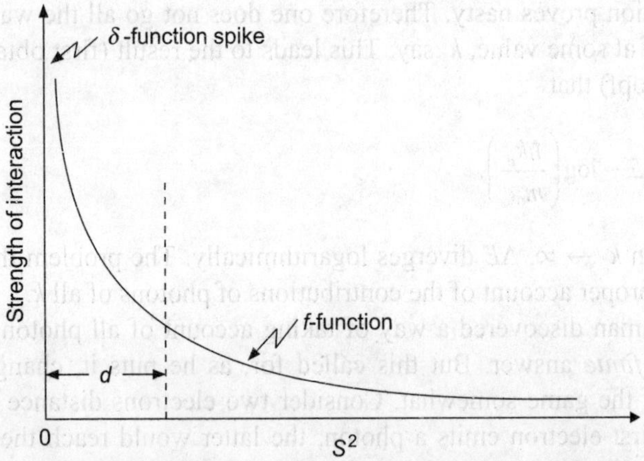

Fig.4.6 Contents of Fig. 4.5 illustrated in a slightly different manner. Explanations in text.

a spike and an exponentially decreasing one. The spike represents the situation when interaction is permitted only when $s^2 = 0$. The technical name for it is δ-function (introduced briefly in Part I), and the interaction is said to be *confined strictly to the light cone*. Feynman stretches it a bit across into the time-like region. The exponential curve which I shall call the *f*-function decays rapidly and soon becomes zero. Therefore when s^2 is sufficiently large, there is really no difference between the standard model and Feynman's fudged model.

How large is large is the next question. And the answer is large means s^2 should be greater than d^2 shown in the figure. Define now $\Lambda = (1/d)$. Using the *f*-function instead of the *f*-function, Feynman is able to integrate over all photons. He then obtains for Δm the result

$$\Delta m = m_0 \frac{3}{2\pi} \frac{e^2}{\hbar c} \left(\log \frac{\hbar \Lambda}{m_0 c} + \frac{1}{4} \right) \tag{4.11}$$

which is a finite number. In other words, using a trick, Feynman is able to comfortably integrate over all k and obtain a finite answer for Δm instead of log ∞ as previous workers (e.g., Weisskopf) did.

Looking at log Λ above, you might be a bit uncomfortable about the whole thing. Really speaking, d should be zero which means $\Lambda = \infty$. Therefore, when we shrink the exponential to approach the spike in Fig.4.6, $\Lambda \rightarrow \infty$ and we have once again a logarithmic infinity! In other words, by introducing Λ, Feynman merely appears to be trading one cutoff for another. Well, you have a point. However, the saving grace is that (i) one can *completely integrate over k* (unlike before) and (ii) get a finite answer for Δm even after making d small ($\sim 10^{-13}$ cm).

As Feynman puts it,

> the prescription for using the f-function instead of the δ-function may be looked upon merely as presenting an *arbitrary rule to cutoff at high frequencies in a relativistically invariant manner*, the otherwise divergent integrals appearing in quantum field theories ... For charges separated by many electron radii $\left(s^2 \gg d^2\right)$ there is essentially no effect of the modification [in going from δ to f]. For the action of an electron on itself, however, there is a considerable modification. The result is/to reduce the infinite self-energy to a finite value.

Feynman himself is aware of the limitations of his prescriptions and remarks:

> Unfortunately, the modifications proposed [$\delta \rightarrow f$] is not completely satisfactory theoretically (it leads to some difficulties of conservation of energy).

Then why push it so hard? Because, after computing Δm according to (4.11), and using it for renormalisation etc., one can eventually let the new cutoff $\Lambda \rightarrow \infty$ and still get a finite answer. To put it differently, after mass correction is made, results for other real processes are finite and insensitive to the width of the cutoff. Hopefully, these last remarks would put you slightly at ease! In passing, you might like to note that ($\hbar\Lambda/c$) is nothing but the regulator mass M_c we met in Chapter 2.

4.10 The physics behind Feynman's approach

In Chapter 1 we saw the crisis faced by classical electromagnetic theory. Later I told you about infinite self-energy in quantum theory and how the problem was fixed. While I described the techniques, I did not devote equal attention to the spirit of the technology and the underlying physics. Time to make amends.

Let us go back to classical theory for a minute. Suppose the electron is a sphere of radius a. Its' self-force F is given by

$$F = \frac{2}{3}\frac{e^2}{ac^2}\dot{v} - \frac{2}{3}\frac{e^2}{c^3}\ddot{v} + \text{other terms.} \tag{4.12}$$

Here we will ignore these other terms and focus just on the first two. The first involves acceleration ($\dot{v}$) and in fact if we ignore the (–2/3) ($e^2\,\ddot{v}/c^3$) term, what we have is just Newton's second law, with of course (2/3) (e^2/ac^2) denoting m_{em} (recall (1.7)).

The second term in (4.12) is quite interesting because it is associated with radiation. As you know, an accelerated charge radiates energy. This electromagnetic field exerts a force

$$F_{rad} = \frac{2}{3}\frac{e^2}{c^3}\ddot{v} \tag{4.13}$$

back on the electron, which is what the second term in (4.12) denotes. Suppose the electron is a point, i.e., we let $a \to 0$. Then the other terms all vanish, F_{rad} survives and the first term blows up. Maybe Maxwell's electrodynamics should be modified so that the idea of a point electron can be maintained without trouble from the self-energy. Many such attempts have in fact been made but all of them have proved unsatisfactory for one reason or another. Even so it is interesting to review some of them in order, as Feynman puts it, "to see the struggles of the human mind."

The simplest thing to do is to say: "Look, there is no such thing as the electron acting on itself." In other words, we set F in (4.12) identically equal to zero. But this does not help any because, as Feynman says, "we have then thrown away the baby with the bath water." Why? because we need F_{rad} and cannot afford to set it equal to zero. The reason is simple. When we accelerate the electron, it radiates energy, i.e., it loses energy. So to accelerate the charge we require more force than we would require for accelerating an uncharged particle. Where does this extra force against which we must do this work, come from? If we consider an empty universe in which there is only one electron which is accelerating, we are forced to the conclusion, that the force comes from the electron itself—perhaps from the action of one part on the other as Lorentz had once said. But then, we are back to square one, especially when we let $a \to 0$. Is there any way in which we can have just F_{rad}, the first term disappearing? No one has found a decent way of doing this, and as Feynman remarks, "classical electron theory has pushed itself into a corner."

One thing which now becomes clear is that when we discuss the force acting on an electron due to itself, we must not only keep in mind the so-called inertial term but also that associated with radiation resistance, i.e., F_{rad}—radiation damping is a fact of life and we cannot afford to ignore it.

In 1938, Dirac suggested a peculiar possibility. He simply postulated that the first term on the r.h.s. of (4.12) is absent and only the second is present. In other words, the electron acts on itself only through F_{rad}. How is this possible? Dirac explained this as follows: Now in Maxwell's theory, when a charge produces a disturbance, the field is propagated as a wave. If the wave leaves the origin (where the disturbance is supposed to be), it would reach a point x at time $t = (x/c)$—the point is that the wave arrives at x later, which makes sense of course. Such a wave-like solution is referred to as a *retarded* wave. Maxwell's equations also admit *advanced* waves as a mathematical solution, i.e., waves which arrive at x at $t = -(x/c)$. But then, who ever heard of waves arriving before they are even emitted? So one customarily ignores the advanced waves. 'Let us symbolically denote these two solutions as W_R and W_A respectively. Dirac pointed out that (4.12) comes from considering W_R only. If W_A is considered then one obtains

$$F = \frac{2}{3}\frac{e^2}{ac^2}\dot{v} - \frac{2}{3}\frac{e^2}{c^3}\ddot{v} \qquad (\text{from } W_A). \tag{4.14}$$

Notice the sign of the second term; it is opposite to that in (4.12). So, Dirac said: Let us make a new rule that the electron acts on itself not via W_R but via (1/2) ($W_R - W_A$). In this case, the force is given by

$$\frac{1}{2}\{(4.12)-(4.14)\} = \frac{2}{3}\frac{e^2}{c^3}\ddot{v}. \tag{4.15}$$

Presto! The inertial term has disappeared but F_{rad} survives. There is no electromagnetic mass, and the classical theory is saved—but at the expense of a weird assumption about the self-force.

Wheeler and Feynman were unhappy with all this. According to the classical theory of the electron as given by Lorentz, for a finite-sized electron the self-force arises due to the action of one part of the electron on another (via W_R). Since the physical radius $a \neq 0$, the self-energy is finite. But then there are problems with relativity. On the other hand, if $a = 0$, the self-energy $\rightarrow \infty$. As far as Dirac is concerned, he certainly got rid of the self-energy problem but his new rule cited above seemed rather arbitrary. In other words, the algorithm was OK but the physics was not clear. So, in the early forties Wheeler and Feynman proposed an even stranger theory according to which point charges interact only with *other* charges. This means there is no such thing as a solitary electron interacting with itself, directly. However, it could interact with other electrons which then interact back. *Thus the presence of other electrons is necessary for back coupling*. In making such a suggestion, Wheeler and Feynman were guided by some thoughts earlier aired by Tetrode (in 1922) who said effectively that an isolated charged particle cannot radiate energy. Energy is emitted only because it can and will be absorbed by another particle! Tetrode put it this way:

> The Sun would not radiate if it were alone in space and no other bodies could absorb its radiation … If, for example, I observed through my telescope yesterday evening that star which let us say is 100 light years away, then not only did I know that the light which it allowed to reach my eye was emitted 100 years ago, but also the star or the individual atoms of it knew already 100 years ago that I, who then did not even exist, would view it yesterday evening at such and such a time …

I am sure you would think Tetrode was out of his mind but the essential point is that the *absorber is an integral part of the mechanism of radiation*. Started this way, Tetrode's idea is not all that crazy. (One is reminded of Newton's bucket experiments and Mach's counter arguments leading to the role played by distant masses etc.; for details, see the companion volume, *At the Speed of Light*.) So, following Tetrode, Wheeler and Feynman assume that

(i) an accelerated point charge in a universe that is otherwise empty does not radiate electromagnetic energy.
(ii) the field which acts on a given particle can arise only from other particles.

I am sure you are quite uneasy. We are trying to understand the force acting on an electron. We are actually interested in the self-force and in particular in F_{rad}. It is now being suggested that there is no such thing as a self-force and that it is all due to other charges in the universe. How on earth is one to calculate that? Wheeler and Feynman show this can be done, without in fact knowing where these so-called "other charges" are. All one has to assume is that the radiation emitted by a moving electron (which we describe as the source) is completely absorbed by these other charges. They then re-radiate. This radiation is described by (1/2) $(W_R + W_A)$. This combines with Dirac's self field described by (1/2) $(W_R - W_A)$ to give a *net field/force associated with* W_R alone, removing all conceptual problems with advanced waves W_A.

So Wheeler and Feynman gave a "handwaving" way of (i) getting rid of the inertial self-force and (ii) explaining F_{rad} in terms of W_R alone. Feynman made this whole business respectable by describing everything from an action principle, i.e., he defined a suitable action S and then demanded it be an extremum.

All this is fine but it is not easy to accept that an electron cannot act on itself. Maybe F_{rad} requires the cooperation of absorbers but the inertial term in (4.12) cannot quite be wished away. However, if one permits the electron to act back on itself, it immediately leads to an infinite self-energy—back to square one! So Feynman decided to rework the theory, starting with an action that incorporated the *f*-function I introduced you to earlier. Result? The self-force is now finite.

So far, everything is classical. Incidentally, it is rather interesting that even here, there is a representation of pair production in the presence of strong fields—see Box 4.2.

Box 4.2 Feynman considered the progress of a classical charged particle from 1 to 2 as illustrated in figure (a). The particle passes through an electrostatic field. The solid line is a path for which the action is an extremum. It is therefore the path the particle would take. It turns out that there is another path, the one shown by the dotted line, for which also the action is an extremum. In this, the particle travels back in time during the segment PQ. One could also interpret it in terms of a pair production at Q and annihilation at P. In other words, there is, within the framework of the above analysis, the possibility of pair production even in classical physics.

(a)

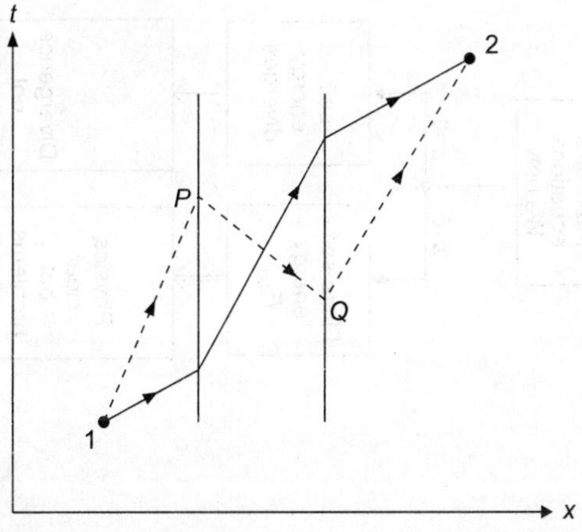

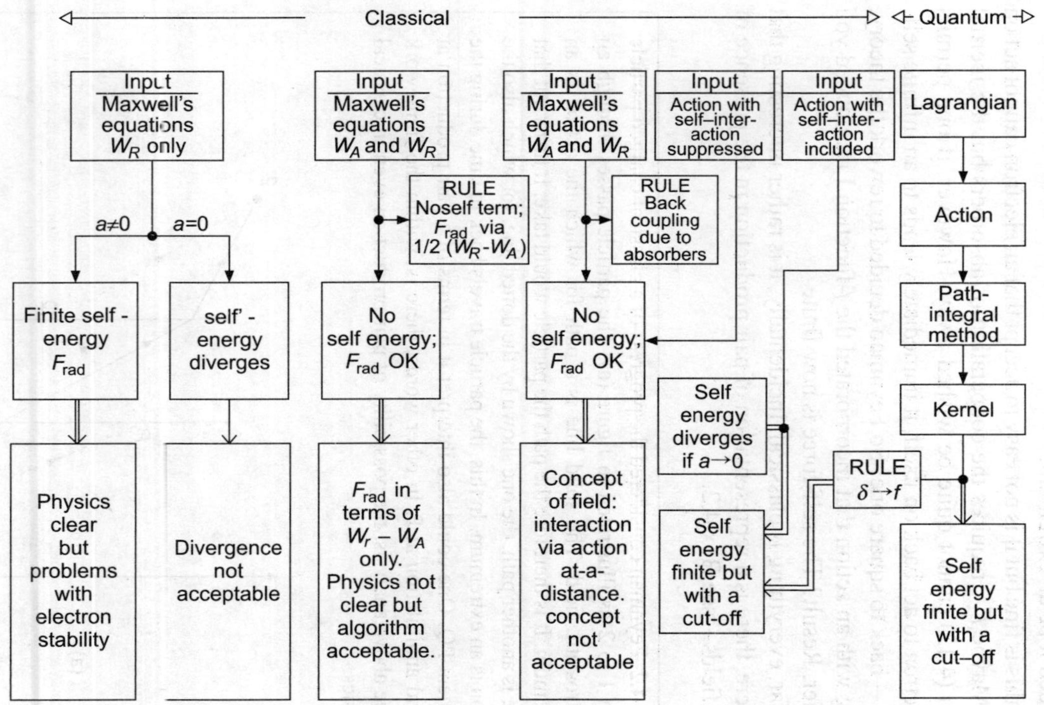

Fig.4.7 Overview of some of the efforts in dealing with the self-energy problem.

The next step obviously would be to carry everything over into quantum theory. But here Feynman ran into a difficulty. Standard QM is not based on an action principle but on the Hamiltonian formalism. For Feynman, however, the Hamiltonian route was unsatisfactory because it got one into trouble with relativistic covariance. And then Feynman stumbled on an old paper by Dirac in which he [Dirac] tried to formulate QM in the action language. This was the lead Feynman was looking for. Latching on to it, he quickly evolved the path integral method. Having now got himself a new style of doing QM, the next step was to apply it to QED. And here he used the $\delta \rightarrow f$ recipe to keep infinities under control. This in brief, is how QED *à* la Feynman evolved.

You would have noticed that in arriving at his version of QED, Feynman went through a series of explorations. First was to develop a classical theory in which an electron cannot interact with itself but only with other electrons. Working with Wheeler, he did it using a combination of advanced and retarded waves. Later he derived it from an action principle. He then found that it really was not necessary to exclude the interaction of an electron with itself. But this brought back the self-energy divergence. However, by the $\delta \rightarrow f$ replacement, the self-energy or the mass increase could be made finite. There remained the task of carrying over these ideas to QM. The path- integral method made this possible. Only, when applying the method to QED, Feynman did not push the Wheeler-Feynman idea. Rather, he stayed with the traditional picture of interaction via retarded waves only, changing, however, the interaction from δ-to f-function. You may say Feynman was daring only to the extent of the $\delta \rightarrow f$ change; the radical Wheeler-Feynman proposal never made it to the quantum world. Figure 4.7 offers an overview of all that I have said so far.

Now for a few "fine print" remarks.

4.11 Renormalisability

Earlier I told you how QED II was a disaster in that it predicted infinites if one stepped beyond the lowest order in perturbation theory. Then I mentioned to you that in QED III this infinity business is kept under check. How? By the counter-term method. I even drew the Feynman diagram associated with this counter term (recall Fig. 3.5). Fine, but *what is the guarantee that all this would, work in higher orders*? In other words, I have made a sales pitch merely by advertising how the infinity is knocked out the first time it raises its head. How does one know it would not give trouble in still higher orders? Good question, and Dyson set all fears to rest by pointing out that the same trick, i.e., renormalisation of a finite number of quantities (mass, charge, electron and photon wave functions) would get rid of all types of infinities in all orders of perturbation theory. One can therefore heave a sigh of relief. A field theory which gives finite answers for all observable phenomena to all orders in perturbation theory via the renormalisation of a finite number of parameters is said to be *renormalisable*. QED is renormalisable.

4.12 Effective propagators and effective vertices

Consider the Feynman diagram in Fig. 4.8(a), and focus on the electron line AB. Between A and B, many things could happen, some examples of which are shown in Figs. 4.8(b), (c), etc. In principle, all these processes must be allowed for. So really speaking, we should replace the "bare" propagator in (a) by an "effective" propagator as in (e).

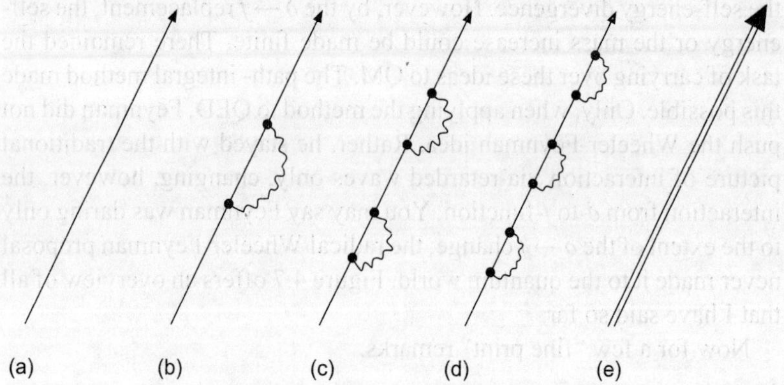

Fig.4.8 Virtual processes and their cumulation into an effective interaction. (a) is for a bare electron while (b), (c), (d) illustrate some virtual processes. The double line in (e) is the effective electron line.

Next let us consider Fig. 4.9. This represents an equation in terms of diagrams. On the right are diagrams which progressively increase in complexity. The cumulative effect of all these processes could be represented in terms of an effective vertex as on the left-hand side.

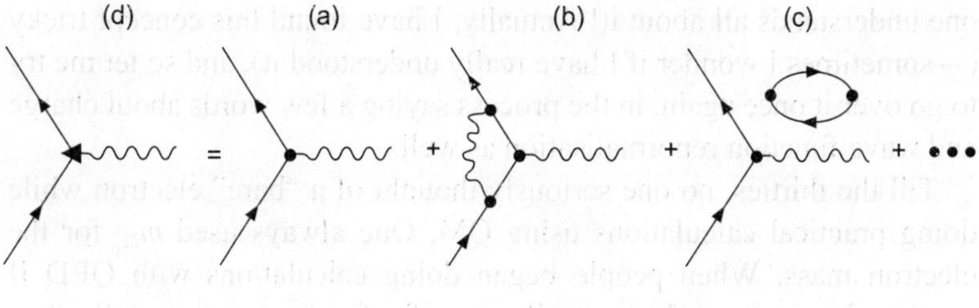

Fig.4.9 Concept of effective vertex illustrated.

We can now make use of concepts like effective propagator and effective vertex to describe physical processes involving real particles. Thus, Compton scattering would be represented by the diagram in Fig. 4.10(b) rather than that in Fig. 4.10(a)—that is when we include all radiative corrections.

You might wonder: "What is there to say that Fig. 4.10(b) is the last word? Why can't one have processes like in Fig. 4.10(c), for example?" This is what Dyson calls including "radiative corrections to radiative corrections and renormalisation of renormalisations, and so on ad infinitum." In a sense, when one draws an effective diagram as in Fig. 4.10(b), these niceties are all taken care of, as far as first-order is concerned of course.

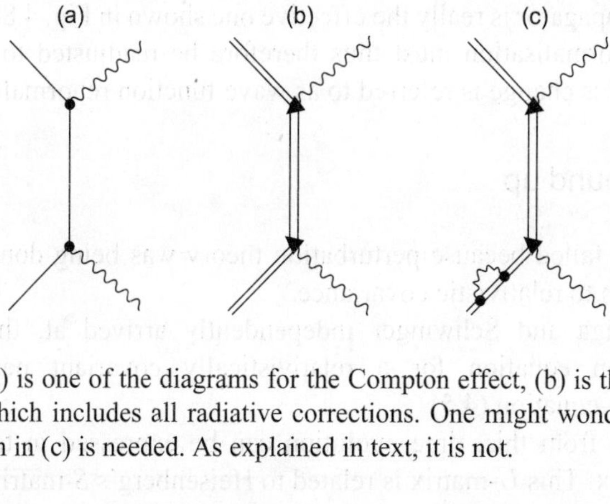

Fig.4.10 (a) is one of the diagrams for the Compton effect, (b) is the effective diagram which includes all radiative corrections. One might wonder whether the diagram in (c) is needed. As explained in text, it is not.

4.13 Mass, charge and wave function renormalisation

I have used the term mass renormalisation several times so far. Familiarity breeds contempt, and one might even begin to feel that one understands all about it! Actually, I have found this concept tricky (—sometimes I wonder if I have really understood it), and so let me try to go over it once again, in the process saying a few words about charge and wave function renormalisation as well.

Till the thirties, no one seriously thought of a "bare" electron while doing practical calculations using QM. One always used $m_{\exp}$ for the electron mass. When people began doing calculations with QED II starting from a bare electron, all sorts of infinities sprang up. So they started going back to basics such as the force exerted by an electron on itself. It was then realised that though in principle one must start with the bare mass m_0, there was not much point in it since we don't anyway know what m_0 is—it is unobservable. So the trick is to replace m_0 by $m_0 + \Delta m$ (mass renormalisation) and kill infinities with a weapon called counter-term.

Just as there is no such thing as a bare mass, there is also no such thing as a bare charge. Like m_0, the bare charge e_0 also is unobservable and so one uses $e = e_0 + \Delta e$ instead of e_0—this is charge renormalisation (see also Section 2.10).

Wave function renormalisation implies something similar. In ordinary (non-relativistic) QM, we do not have virtual processes and all that. The free electron propagator is thus as shown in Fig.4.8(a), and the wave function is normalised keeping this scenario in mind. However, we know that the propagator is really the effective one shown in Fig. 4.8(e). Wave function normalisation must thus therefore be readjusted to this new scenario; this change is referred to as wave function renormalisation.

4.14 A round up

- QED II failed because perturbation theory was being done without attention to relativistic covariance.
- Tomonaga and Schwinger independently arrived at. the correct evolution equation for a relativistically covariant perturbation theory—equation (4.5).
- Starting from this, time evolution can be expressed in terms of a U-matrix. This U-matrix is related to Heisenberg's S-matrix.
- More important, equation (4.9) shows how the U-matrix forms the foundation stone for a perturbation theory.
- In the Schwinger-Tomonaga version, the perturbing Hamiltonian is in the interaction representation.

- Feynman's approach is an integral approach as compared to the Schwinger–Tomonaga differential approach—see (4.7).
- It is a product of his path-integral method of doing QM. Feynman finds this convenient for ensuring relativistic covariance.
- At the working level, Feynman treats the past and future in a symmetric fashion. His method therefore corresponds to the use of a "mixed" representation as opposed to the interaction representation.

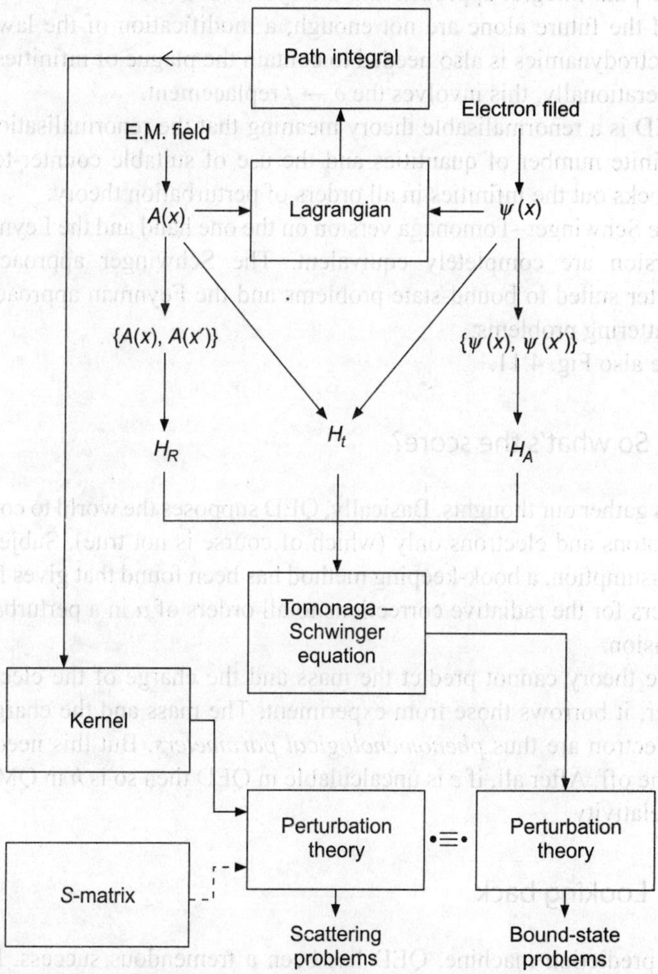

Fig.4.11 Flow chart giving an overview of the approaches of Feynman on the one hand and Schwinger–Tomonaga on the other.

- Operationally, allowing the past and future to coexist enables electrons to go back in time. This not only permits mimicking the positron but allows consideration of paths and their relative amplitudes in the spirit of a path-integral approach.
- Treating the past and the future in a symmetric fashion is an echo of a paper by Wheeler and Feynman in which both advanced and retarded waves were used.
- The path-integral approach and the symmetric treatment of the past and the future alone are not enough; a modification of the laws of electrodynamics is also needed to contain the plague of infinities.
- Operationally, this involves the $\delta \rightarrow f$ replacement.
- QED is a renormalisable theory meaning that the renormalisation of a finite number of quantities and the use of suitable counter-terms knocks out the infinities in all orders of perturbation theory.
- The Schwinger–Tomonaga version on the one hand and the Feynman version are completely equivalent. The Schwinger approach is better suited to bound-state problems and the Feynman approach to scattering problems.
- See also Fig. 4.11.

4.15 So what's the score?

Let us gather our thoughts. Basically, QED supposes the world to consist of photons and electrons only (which of course is not true). Subject to this assumption, a book-keeping method has been found that gives finite answers for the radiative corrections to all orders of α in a perturbation expansion.

The theory cannot predict the mass and the charge of the electron. Rather, it borrows those from experiment. The mass and the charge of the electron are thus *phenomenological parameters*. But this need not put one off. After all, if e is uncalculable in QED then so is h in QM and c in relativity.

4.16 Looking back

As a prediction machine, QED has been a tremendous success. Does this mean people are completely satisfied with it? Not really. Here is a sample of opinions.

Dyson

Tomonaga, Schwinger and Feynman rescued the theory without making any radical innovations. Their victory was a victory for conservatism. They kept the physical basis of the theory precisely as it had been laid down by Dirac, and only changed the mathematical superstructure. By polishing and refining with great skill the mathematical formalism, they were able to show that the theory does in fact give meaningful predictions for all observable quantities. The predictions in all cases are finite, unambiguous, and in agreement with experiment. The divergent and meaningless quantities are indeed present in the theory but they appear in a way that they automatically eliminate themselves from any quantity which is in principle observable...

The theory as Tomonaga, Schwinger and Feynman left it has stood the test of time. It describes only a part of physical reality, and it makes no claim to finality. The present electrodynamics is certainly incomplete, but it is no longer certainly incorrect.

Feynman

The shell game that we play ... is technically called "renormalisation". But no matter how clever the word, it is what I would call a dippy process! Having to resort to such hocus-pocus has prevented us from proving that the theory of quantum electrodynamics is mathematically self-consistent ... I suspect that renormalisation is not mathematically legitimate ... I believe there is really no satisfactory quantum electrodynamics, but I am not sure ... I think that the renormalisation theory is simply a way to sweep difficulties of divergences of electrodynamics under the rug. I am, of course not sure of that!

Schwinger

It is not likely that future developments will drastically change the results of the electron theory. [However] this physically incomplete theory [QED III] suffers from a fundamental limitation. It can never explain the observed value of the dimensionless coupling constant [α] ... A full understanding of the electron charge can exist only when the theory of elementary particles has come to a stage of perfection that is presently unimaginable.

Dirac

Recent work by Lamb, Schwinger and Feymnan and others has been very successful ... but the resulting theory is an ugly and incomplete one.

Schweber

It could be argued that ... both Feynman's and Schwinger's formulations although technically more manageable and much superior, were not major advances in *physical content* over the quantum field theory of the '30s [i.e., QED II]. The question to be answered is why the post-World War II generation, unlike the generation of the '30s, was successful in bypassing the obstacles posed by quantum field theory ... The workers of the '30s—Heisenberg, Bohr, Rosenfeld, Pauli, Dirac—all sought solutions of the problems in terms of *revolutionary* departures (e.g., non-positive metrics in Hilbert space and new fundamental lengths). Special relativity and quantum mechanics had been advanced by such revolutionary steps, and in the '30s Bohr constantly advocated and encouraged such attitudes for the solution of the field-theoretic problems. The solution of Feynman, Schwinger and Dyson was in essence conservative; it asked to take seriously the received formulation of quantum mechanics and special relativity and to explore the content of this synthesis. A generational conflict manifested itself in this contrast between the revolutionary and conservative stances of the pre- and post-World War II generations.

Weisskopf

The war against infinities was ended. There was no reason any more to fear higher-order terms. The renormalisation took care of all infinities and provides an unambiguous way to calculate with any desired accuracy any phenomena resulting from the coupling of the electrons with the electromagnetic field. It was not a complete victory, because infinite counter-terms had to be reintroduced to remove the infinities. Furthermore, the procedure of eliminating infinities could be carried out only by renormalising successively at each step of the perturbation expansion in powers of the coupling parameter. It is still not clear whether this method leads to a convergent series. It is like Hercules' fight against Hydra, the many-headed monster, which grows a new head for every one cut off. But Hercules won his fight and so did the physicists. Sydney Drell characterised the situation most aptly as "a peaceful coexistence with the infinities".

Wightman

There are three reasons why a theory dependant on cutoff methods must be regarded as fundamentally unsatisfactory. First, physical processes can occur at all energies, no matter how high ... Second, the higher the cutoff, the larger are the correction factors for particle mass and charge ... Third, and the most disconcerting of all, ... the resulting formalism cannot be guaranteed to be consistent.

4.17 Concluding remarks

The message is clear: QED works but is intellectually not satisfying. So what's to be done? Some people believe that the root of the problem lies in classical electrodynamics. Perhaps that should be straightened out first. If quantum modifications are made afterwards, we would get a neat and elegant replacement for what we have now. Dirac was one of those who strongly felt this way, and so he went back to restructuring the classical theory of the electron. As he put it:

> A new physical idea is needed which should be intelligible both in the classical theory and in the quantum theory and our easiest path of approach is to keep within the confines of the classical theory.

Dirac made several attempts to come up with such a theory but did not succeed.

While QED itself might be accepted only with reservation, not so the "third way of doing QM" pioneered by Feynman, i.e., the path-integral method. About it Murray Gell-Mann says:

> The path-integral formulation of quantum mechanics may be more fundamental than the conventional one, in that there is a crucial domain where it may apply and the conventional formulation may fail. That domain is quantum cosmology.

5 The Principal Actors

SIN-ITIRO TOMONAGA

Sin-Itiro Tomonaga was born in Japan in 1906. He grew up in Kyoto where his father was a Professor of Philosophy at the Imperial University. In 1929, Tomonaga obtained the Bachelor's degree from the Kyoto University. One of his batchmates was Hideki Yukawa, who later won the Nobel Prize for his prediction of the meson. For three years after graduation, both Yukawa and Tomonaga worked as unpaid assistants in the University. Yukawa then found an opening in the physics department but Tomonaga could not. Later, he also got a break. In 1931, Yoshio Nishina (later to become well known) visited Kyoto to deliver a series of lecture on the Dirac theory, which both Yukawa and Tomonaga attended. Nishina was actually trained in electrical engineering. In 1917, he joined the Institute for Physical and Chemical Research, the Rikagaku Kenkyusho-Riken. After a long spell at Riken, Nishina went to Europe where he spent many years, visiting various laboratories. And it was during his stay at the Bohr institute that he worked on the famous Klein – Nishina formula.

Nishina noticed that Tomonaga and Yukawa were keen listeners. Since Yukawa already had a job, Nishina offered a research assistant's position to Tomonaga which the latter gladly accepted. So this brought Tomonaga to Tokyo in 1932, and naturally Tomonaga and Nishina began to work together. To start with, it was on problems in nuclear physics but once the positron was discovered, their interest was aroused by quantum electrodynamics.

In 1937, Tomonaga went to Leipzig to study under and work with Heisenberg. He stayed there for two years and used the results obtained while working there to write up a thesis for the Tokyo University. He submitted this on his return to Japan, and was awarded the doctorate degree in 1940. The following year he was appointed Professor of Physics in Tokyo University. And it was during this period that he did his most famous work, namely the relativistically covariant formulation of quantum field theory.

Meanwhile the Second World War intervened and Tomonaga drifted to war-oriented work. After the war, he resumed his research in quantum electrodynamics, spurred of course by the discovery of the Lamb shift. The Japanese group headed by Tomonaga worked under a great handicap. Not only was Japan cut off from the scientific happenings elsewhere, but life itself was difficult in a nation which had just suffered a heavy and humiliating defeat. If anything, their work shows that perseverance always gets rewarded, no matter what the circumstances. In Tomonaga's case, his work received immediate acclaim in America, though he belonged to a country which just a short time earlier had been its bitter enemy.

It is particularly interesting that the person who helped to bring Tomonaga's contributions to the notice of the American and the world scientific community was none other than Robert Oppenheimer, the leader of the Manhattan project which was set up to build the atomic bomb. Later, Oppenheimer invited Tomonaga to spend some time at the Institute for Advanced Study in Princeton of which he (Oppenheimer) was the Director.

In later years, Tomonaga won many honours including the Nobel Prize. He also occupied important positions in the academic world. He passed away in 1970.

JULIAN SCHWINGER

Julian Schwinger was born in 1918 in New York, three months before Feynman. He was a child prodigy, with an extraordinary flair for mathematics and a photographic memory. He finished high school at 15 and started attending the theoretical physics seminar at Columbia University where Rabi, later to win the Nobel Prize for his work on atomic beams, was in-charge. Young Schwinger caught the attention of Rabi by his intelligent comments during the seminars. Rabi then offered Schwinger a scholarship. By the time he received the B.A. degree in 1936, Schwinger had not only written many papers on the scattering of neutrons from hydrogen but had even completed his Ph.D. thesis! However, he had to wait another two years to complete all the formal course requirements before be became eligible to receive the doctorate degree.

After obtaining the Ph.D. degree, Schwinger worked for brief periods in various universities in America. In 1943, he joined the

Massachusetts Institute of Technology (MIT) as a member of the faculty and worked on problems related to radar. In 1945 he joined Harvard University as Associate Professor of Physics, and two years later he was appointed full Professor. He was then 29, the youngest Professor in Harvard. In 1965, he shared the Nobel Prize along with Tomonaga and Feynman.

Schwinger was a mathematical virtuoso. His papers left one dazed and ordinary mortals retreated after paying their respects. Reflecting on this, Dyson has observed, "An unkind critic once said: Other people publish to show how to do it, but Julian Schwinger publishes to show you that only he can do it." Schwinger has defended himself against such criticism with the remark, "I gather I stand accused of presenting a finished elaborate mathematical formalism from which had been excised all the physical insights that provide signposts to its construction. To all charges I plead Not Guilty."

Unfortunately, biographical material about Schwinger is somewhat scarce. Some more material about him may be found in Chapter 6. As of now, he is the sole survivor of the original trio.

RICHARD FEYNMAN

We now come to Feynman, unquestionably the most colourful of the three founding fathers of modern QED. He is also perhaps the best known, thanks to his writings, lectures, etc. Not surprisingly, he has been quoted several times in this series of books.

Compared to Tomonaga and Schwinger, a lot more biographical material about Feynman is available, thanks especially to his two books *Surely you're Joking Mr. Feynman* and *What do you care what others say* ? These books are so well known that I shall skip the usual biographical notes in this case. Instead, I shall supplement with some material that is perhaps not so well known.

Let me start with a thumbnail sketch. Born, 1918 in New York state. Got his Bachelor's degree from MIT in 1939. Joined Princeton University to do a Ph.D. with John Wheeler as advisor. Meanwhile war broke out and Feynman went to Los Alamos to work on the atom bomb project (Project Manhattan). In between, collected his Ph.D. from Princeton in 1942. After the war went to Cornell University. In 1950 moved to the California Institute of Technology (Caltech). In 1959 became the Richard Chance Tolman Professor. Underwent a major operation for cancer around late 1979. Passed away in 1988.

Feynman was a remarkable personality. When he died, the famous newspaper *The New York Times* wrote:

> Hans Bethe of Cornell University said there were two kinds of geniuses. The ordinary kind does great things but lets other scientists feel that they could do the same if only they worked hard enough. The other kind performs magic.
>
> A magician does things that nobody else could ever do and that seems completely unexpected; and that's Feynman.

We start with Feynman as he is about to enter the Princeton University as a graduate (i.e., Ph.D.) student. When Feynman's application was received, the Admission Committee went into raptures. Let me quote Wheeler at this point.

> "This chap from MIT. Look at his aptitude test ratings in mathematics and physics. Fantastic! ... He must be a diamond in the rough..."
>
> These are not the exact words, but they convey the flavour of the Committee discussions...

Graduate students earn money by assisting professors in their teaching. Feynman was assigned to help Wheeler in a course on mechanics, and one day they got into a discussion about the automatic lawn sprinkler. This is a device used commonly for watering the lawn. About this discussion Wheeler recalls:

> Shaped like a swastika, it [the sprinkler] shoots out four jets of water. The recoil drives the sprinkler arms round and round. But where does the recoil act? Doesn't it act at the point where the stream of water suddenly changes direction from straight out to straight transverse? But suppose the arm sucks water in instead of squirting it out. Surely, we said to each other, there is an identical change in direction and therefore an identical reaction. Surely the sprinkler will again turn around when water in the arms is sucked in rather than being shot out. Oh no, it won't. Oh yes, it will. We had a great time trying out both sides of the question on our colleagues. As the days went by, more and more colleagues up and down the corridor took positions. The debate grew more animated ... The situation called for an experiment.
>
> Feynman made a six-inch miniature lawn Sprinkler out of glass tubing and hung it from a flexible tube of rubber. He checked that it

> worked OK as a sprinkler. Then he wangled the whole dangling gadget through the throat of a great glass carboy filled with water. He got this outfit set up on the floor of the cyclotron lab, where there was a handy compressed-air outlet. He ran the compressed air in through a second hole in the cork at the top of the carboy. Ha! A little tremor as the pressure was first applied, as the water first began to run backward through the miniature lawn sprinkler. But, as the flow continued there was no reaction. Then increase the air pressure. Get more backward flow of water. Again a momentary tremor at the start of this manoeuvre but no continuing torque. OK, more pressure. And more! Boom! The glass container exploded. Water and fragments of glass went all over the cyclotron room. From that time onward Feynman was banished from the lab!

All this might appear like a childish prank. On the other hand, it reveals Feynman's attitude to learning. Though he was a theorist, he was never a pencil-and-paper man. In fact, in marked contrast to many celebrated theorists he not only respected experiments but also experimentalists. Prof. Telegdi of Chicago comments:

> "He gave us experimentalists (or gave us back?) our dignity. This he did in two ways. He emphasised that physics was an experimental science and hence would dry up without facts. He understood experiments deeply and could suggest sources of error that had escaped the experimenters themselves. Being questioned by him was a harrowing experience. Beyond that, he gave us the assurance, by ripping away the mask of formalism from the face of simple facts, that we too could understand the deeper meaning and significance of our own work. To him, as to Enrico Fermi, the difference between a theorist and an experimenter was one of technique primarily and not one of intellectual competence.

Feynman was not only an outstanding physicist but also an outstanding lecturer. In fact he was an actor as well, as can be sensed from the famous lecture series of his and his more popular books like *The Character of the Physical Law* and *QED*. People who have heard him simply rave about him. Here is an example of his showmanship cited by David Goodstein, a colleague at Caltech.

> I can remember many moments of high drama in Feynman lectures. Once, for example, several years ago, he taught a course in advanced quantum mechanics in a large lecture hall, to a class consisting of a

> few registered graduate students and most of the Caltech physics faculty. At one point he started explaining how to represent complicated integrals diagrammatically: time on this axis, space on that axis, wiggly line for this, straight line for that and ... turning around suddenly to face the class with a wicked grin he said, "and this is called *the diagram*!" The class ignited with spontaneous applause.

About Feynman's ability to make physics come alive, Freeman Dyson says:

> His most valuable contribution to physics is as a sustainer of morale; when he bursts into the room with his latest brain-wave and proceeds to expound it with most lavish sound effects and waving about of arms, life at least is not dull.

Nobel Prize winner Murray Gell-Mann with whom Feynman has collaborated confirms this view.

> He [Feynman] was a picture of energy, vitality and playfulness. That was Richard at his best.
>
> He often worked on theoretical physics in the same way, with zest and humour. When we were together discussing physics, we would exchange ideas and silly jokes in between bouts of mathematical calculation—we struck sparks off each other, and it was exhilarating.
>
> What I always liked about Richard's style was the lack of pomposity in his presentation. I was tired of theorists who dressed up their work in fancy mathematical language or invented pretentious frameworks for their sometimes rather modest contributions. Richard's ideas, often powerful, ingenious and original, were presented in a straightforward manner that I found refreshing.

It is not merely while discussing physics or while lecturing on it that Feynman was strikingly different. He was so in real life too. His house was full of all sorts of animals and once he obliged his neighbour by agreeing to take care of her pet snake, a boa constrictor (this is the South American equivalent of our python)! About this, Dyson says:

> I heard later from Feynman that this affair with the boa constrictor ended badly. Feynman was responsible for the care and the feeding of the boa constrictor. The trouble was that the boa constrictor was supposed to eat live white mice, but when Feynman fed him the mice he was too stupid or lazy to catch them. Instead of the boa constrictor eating the mice, the mice began eating the boa constrictor.

> So Feynman had to sit up at night to stop the mice from nibbling holes in the boa constrictor's skin. And when the owner of the boa constrictor came back, she scolded Feynman for taking care of the animal so badly.

Dyson recalls another incident which again reveals Feynman as a highly individualistic and an unusual personality.

> We were together at a small meeting of physicists organised by John Wheeler at the University of Texas [this was in 1981, just a few years before Feynman died]. For some reason, Wheeler decided to hold this meeting at a grotesque place called the World of Tennis, a country club where Texas millionaires go to relax. So there we were. We grumbled at the high prices and the extravagant ugliness of our rooms. But there was nowhere else to go. Or so we thought. But Dick [Richard Feynman] thought otherwise. Dick just said: "To hell with it. I am not going to sleep in this place," picked up his suitcase and walked off alone into the woods. In the morning he reappeared, looking none the worse for his night under the stars. He said that he did not sleep much, but it was worth it.

We come to the last phase of Feynman's life when he spent sometime working in a computer company called *Thinking Machines Corporation*. This Company builds what are called massively parallel computers, and was started by one Daniel Hillis. Rather interesting that Hillis started thinking about forming a company even while he was a Ph.D. student. Hillis describes how Feynman came to his company.

> I got to know Richard [Feynman] through his son. Carl was one of the undergraduates helping me with my thesis project. I was trying to design a computer fast enough to solve commonsense reasoning problems. The machine, as we envisioned it, would include a million tiny computers, all connected by a communications network. We called it the *Connection Machine* ...
>
> One day in the spring of 1983, when I was having lunch with Richard Feynman I mentioned to him that I was planning to start a company to build a parallel computer with a million processors. His reaction was unequivocal: "That is positively the dopiest idea I ever heard." For Richard, a crazy idea was an opportunity to prove it wrong—or to prove it right. Either way, he was interested. By the end of lunch he had agreed to spend summer working at the company.

Now the fun starts. Feynman was dead serious about working in Hillis' company, and sure enough he showed up in Boston (where the company was) as soon as it was started. Hillis recalls:

> We were arguing about what the name of the company should be when Richard walked in, saluted and said, "Richard Feynman reporting for duty. OK, boss, what's my assignment?"
>
> The assembled group of not-quite-graduated MIT students was astounded. After a hurried private discussion ("I don't know, you hired him ..."), we informed Richard that his assignment would be to advise on the application of parallel processing to scientific problems. "That sounds like a bunch of baloney," he said. "Give me something real to do."
>
> So we sent him out to buy some office supplies. [Imagine sending a Nobel Prize winner out on an errand like that!] While he was gone, we decided that the part of the machine we were most worried about was the router that delivered messages from one processor to another.

That's what Hillis and others decided Feynman must tackle and that's how Feynman got started. Unfortunately, I cannot describe the various incidents that involved Feynman in the above-mentioned computer company but I must mention one or two things to bring forth aspects of his personality. Back to Hillis again:

> I had never managed a big group before, and I was clearly in over my head. Richard volunteered to help out. "We've got to get these guys organised," he told me. "Let me tell you how we did it at Los Alamos."

For Feynman, the atomic bomb project at Los Alamos was the ultimate in doing complex projects in an organised way. Feynman's appreciation for and emphasis on organisation is most interesting because most theoretical physicists are loners by temperament and do not ever bother about such "mundane" matters.

For Feynman, getting organised meant many things. For instance, he arranged for many experts to visit the company and give seminars. By injecting a strong academic flavour, Feynman helped the computer designers to think in the most modern and in a completely unconventional way—after all, the name of the company was Thinking Machines Corporation!

Another major contribution (non technical that is, for Feynman also made many innovative technical contributions) was how to put ideas across and explain technical things to non experts. Here the regular designers tended to perform very poorly, drowning the poor listener with a lot of mumbo jumbo. Feynman would take over, simplify everything and state facts in words that the audience would understand. As Hillis recalls:

> It [Feynman's simplified explanation of technical work done by company professionals] infuriated the experts who had worked on the problem because it did not even mention all of the clever problems that they had solved. On the other hand, it delighted the listeners because they could walk away with a real understanding of the calculation [this refers to the calculations performed using the company's parallel computer] and how it was connected to physical reality.
>
> We tried to take advantage of Richard's talent for clarity by getting him to criticise the technical presentations we made in our product introductions. Before the commercial announcement of the first Connection Machine, CM-1, and all of our subsequent products, Richard would give a sentence-by-sentence critique of the planned presentation. "Don't say 'reflected acoustic wave.' Say echo Or, "Forget all that local minima stuff. Just say there's a bubble caught in the crystal and you have to shake it out." Nothing made him angrier than making something simple sound complicated.

Well, there's a lesson for many of us! All this may tend to give the impression that Feynman was just a great showman. No question he was one but that should not hide something much deeper. Former student Brown expresses it as follows:

> It [Feynman's showmanship etc.] leaves out so much; not only his scientific genius, but his deep love of Nature, his passion for teaching, and above all his extraordinary standards of personal integrity, not *always* present at the highest levels of creativity ... Whatever else Dick Feynman might have joked about, his love for physics approached reverence.

6 How It All Happened

This is a difficult chapter because I have to weave several different stories into one unified account. It seems best to start with the discovery made by Willis E. Lamb Jr. which, in a sense, was the turning point.

6.1 The discovery of Lamb shift

Lamb says that his first "contact" with the fine structure of hydrogen was his meeting with Michelson during a chess tournament in 1929 in California. At that time Lamb was a school student and Michelson a guest at the tournament because he too was an avid chess fan. For more about Michelson, see the companion volume *At the Speed of Light.*

In 1930, Lamb went to Berkeley to study chemistry. Gilbert Lewis was the Dean. To him goes the credit for naming the light quantum, as the photon. Lamb says,

> He advised me to become an experimentalist rather than a theorist. The reason was that a theorist without a good idea was useless, whereas an experimentalist could always go into the laboratory and "polish up the brass."

Soon physics seemed more interesting to Lamb and he made a switch, joining Oppenheimer as a student. About Oppenheimer, Lamb recalls:

> Oppenheimer's office was room 219, Le Comte Hall. As were many of his students, I was given a small table in the room. Oppenheimer had no desk but only a table in the middle of the room, heavily strewn with papers. One wall was covered with a blackboard and hardly ever erased. One set of open shelves had reprints of Oppenheimer's publications. I was allowed to have a copy of most of these. In one paper, which impressed me mightily, Oppenheimer pointed out specifically for the first time how the quantum electrodynamics of

> Dirac, Werner Heisenberg, and Wolfgang Pauli led to self-energy divergence difficulties. This paper was written before the reinterpretation of the negative energy states, and consequently the divergences were not as manageable as they were later to become. His attempt to subtract one infinite integral from another did not succeed. Despite this, Oppenheimer noted that a judicious selection of some of the integrals for the infinite energy of the $2P$ state of hydrogen led to a finite result. Hall carried out the necessary calculations and obtained a $2S_{1/2} - 2P_{1/2}$ level shift of 1,700 MHz. This wasn't really a meaningful procedure, but it was certainly a suggestive one, although few people took it seriously or remembered it.

After obtaining the Ph.D. in 1938, Lamb went to Columbia University as an instructor. Rabi was the presiding deity and things were hectic in his laboratory. There were many students and Lamb remembers:

> Another student seen only during the night hours, Julian Schwinger, was already making major contributions to theoretical physics …
>
> My teaching load was only 12 hours per week … This left me plenty of time for research …

Lamb started by completing the work he had commenced earlier in California on the resonant capture of neutrons by nuclei embedded in solids. Two decades later, Rudolph Mössbauer, leaning heavily on this paper, explained the resonant capture of gamma rays by nuclei embedded in solids and went on to win the Nobel Prize. Meanwhile the war intervened, and many scientists disappeared to participate in the war effort. Lamb remained at Columbia University and after a while joined the war effort in the University itself. He was assigned to work in the Columbia Radiation Laboratory (CRL). About it Lamb says:

> This laboratory was housed on one and later two floors of the physics building. There was an armed guard day and night. The main work at CRL involved microwave magnetron oscillators. This stimulated me many years later to develop theories of maser and laser devices…
>
> Although my main job at the CRL was to provide theory, sometimes I would think of an experimental configuration for a magnetron device that interested me. I could not hope to get anyone who was involved in the serious business of designing, building, and testing

> magnetrons to waste time on my ideas. I could, if I wished, build anything I wanted with the help of the superb shop facilites, as long as I carried on the fabrication myself ..., I did not know anything of metal fabrication, high-vacuum techniques, etc. ... I gradually learned the things I needed to know in order to make a few special kinds of magnetron devices...

It seemed as if Lamb was destined to discover the Lamb shift. One is tempted to draw this conclusion from what Lamb himself says:

> During this whole time I continued to teach. In particular, I taught a course in atomic physics in the summer session of 1945. The textbook assigned was Herzberg's *Atomic Spectra and Atomic Structure*. I found in this book a reference to the selection rules for allowed optical transitions in atomic hydrogen. It seemed that the wavelength for a transition between the fine-structure terms for $n = 2$ would have a wavelength of abou 3 cm. ... I was struck by the near equality of this wavelength and that of my magnetrons ...
>
> I felt now that I had something to think about! ... All I had to do was to learn how to make gas discharges that could produce activated hydrogen atoms and measure the absorption of microwaves as a function of the wavelength. Such thoughts came into and out of my mind for a good part of the year.

We now come to the most interesting part of Lamb's recollections.

> The war was over, but work continued on various projects at CRL, and we hoped that some of its research could continue in peace time ... In 1945, I was given a promotion to assistant professor ... I continued to think intermittently about how one might make a microwave measurement of the hydrogen fine structure. By July of 1946, I had some vague ideas of what to try, and I even placed an order in the shops for the parts of a crude apparatus ... Just at this time, Robert Retherford decided to return to Columbia as a graduate [Ph.D.] student. He had begun his research before the war on atomic beams with Kellogg but had gone off to work on vacuum tubes for Westing-house. He was an ideal partner for the project now increasingly dear to my heart ...
>
> The experiment first succeeded on Saturday, April 26, 1947, and turned out to be very much as expected except for the location of the resonances ... I remember that late that night after Retherford had gone home, I went to the laboratory to see if I could confirm

> the earlier results … I awakened the following morning with the realization that a very nice experiment had worked. It made for a very good feeling. I realised that the research was of a quality deserving a Nobel Prize.

Many of the interested persons were duly informed, and congratulations poured in. But somehow Lamb forgot to inform Dirac, and about this he recalls:

> In 1959 I had a walk with Dirac around the island of Mainau in Lake Constance. He told me that he had learned of the microwave measurements through a clipping from the front page of *The New York Times*. It is clear that I should have sent him the news in a more direct manner.

Sommerfeld, the grand old man of modern spectroscopy was 81 at that time but active enough still to appreciate the discovery and send Lamb a congratulatory note. Lamb has another Dirac story.

> In the sixties I shared a bus ride with Dirac at a conference in Lindau [Nobel Laureates used to meet from time to time at Lindau]. He asked me if I enjoyed participating in the discovery of the fine structure anomaly. I replied yes, but indicated I would have had much more pleasure if instead I could have discovered his relativistic wave equation. After a brief pause, he said gently, "Things were simpler then."

6.2 The Shelter Island Conference

In June 1947, there was a conference arranged by Oppenheimer where Lamb reported his results. It immediately had an electrifying impact. So let us now turn to this conference, which is often referred to as the Shelter Island Meeting/Conference. About it Rabi later said, "It would be remembered as the Solvay Congress of 1911 is remembered, for having been the starting point of remarkable new developments," while Feynman recalled, "There have been conferences in the world since, but I have never felt any to be as important as this."

The background to this historic meeting goes back to late 1945 when Duncan MacInnes of the Rockefeller Institute and a former President of the New York Academy of Sciences went to see Frank Jewett, head of the National Academy of Sciences about organising specialised science conferences. The war was over, and science had to get moving again. Scientists had to come together, discuss, and exchange ideas. Conferences provided a good forum for all this but the existing conferences had become too big and unwieldy—I wonder what MacInnes would think of some of today's meetings!—as a result of which serious exchange of ideas was becoming impossible. Jewett agreed but desired that conferences should focus on real problems and that their solutions "could be aided by the concentrated consideration of a small highly qualified group meeting in intimate association for discussion after study of the prepared papers ... A two or three day meeting at some quiet place where the men could live together intimately seemed the best way to obtain the desired results."

Encouraged, MacInnes chose two topics: The Nature of Biopotential and The Postulates of Quantum Mechanics. Concerning the latter, MacInnes consulted K.K. Darrow of Bell Labs who talked to Brillouin who in turn recommended that advice be sought from Pauli then in Princeton. Pauli wanted the title changed to The Fundamental Problems of Quantum Mechanics. He also gave a long list of names of big shots, mostly European. MacInnes was quite unhappy about these suggestions because his idea was to bring together young American physicists rather than old European physicists. He was even more upset when in February 1946, Pauli and Wheeler wrote to him suggesting that the conference proposed by him be merged with one Bohr was planning in Copenhagen in December 1947.

Darrow now got into the act once again, and made it clear to Wheeler that the MacInnes' proposal was to have an *American* conference "to bring out" the young American theoretical physicists who had played such a large role in the successful war effort. More consultations followed and by March 1946 some sort of a consensus emerged. The proposed conference would deal with problems connected with the quantum mechanics of the electron, attendance would be limited, young people would find a place, and the meeting would be in some quiet country inn. The total budget would be $ 3,120, covering a two-day stay for 30 people, travel expenses for people coming from a distance, secretarial assistance, postage, proceedings, etc. At today's prices, this seems unbelievable! MacInnes was happy he had prevented "the capture of the conference by the other group."

In February 1947, Jewett gave MacInnes the final green signal to go ahead. With the help of John Denning, Regional Manager of the Department of Commerce of the State of New York, Ram's Head Inn at Shelter Island near New York was selected. This island was a holiday resort and sufficiently isolated. In early April, invitations to attend the conference were mailed to 25 people identified by Rabi and Darrow, based on various suggestions they had received. Kramers, Oppenheimer and Weisskopf were to be the discussion leaders. It is interesting that seven of the participants were later to receive the Nobel Prize!

The participants were asked to assemble in the offices of the American Physical Society in New York on Sunday 1, June 1947 from where they were taken by "an old and shaky bus" to a village called Green-port. About the last part of this bus ride, Abraham Pais a participant has this to say:

> As we entered Nassau County, the bus was stopped by a police trooper on a motor cycle who asked: "Are you scientists?" Yes, we are scientists. "Follow me", he said to the driver, escorting us to the tune of sirens, to Suffolk County where other troopers took over. We had no clue as to what this meant and speculated about security measures which in those days did tend to take bizarre forms. All was cleared up after a dinner offered at Greenport when a kindly gentleman rose and said that the escort was appreciative of what "the scientists" had meant in his own life. He had been a Marine in the Pacific and might not have been there to thank us had it not been for the atomic bomb. After a ferry ride to Ram's island, we settled down.

Darrow was supposed to be the conference chairman but it was Oppenheimer who dominated the proceedings. In his diary Darrow wrote:

> As the conference went on, the ascendency of Oppenheimer became more evident—the analysis (often caustic) of nearly every argument, that magnificent English never marred by hesitation or the groping for words (I never heard "catharsis" used in a discourse on physics), the dry humour, the perpetually recurring comment that one idea or another (including his own) was wrong, and the respect with which he was heard.

One of the discussion leaders at Shelter Island was Weisskopf. Fully familiar with the divergence difficulties (of QED II), Weisskopf identified the removal of infinities as priority number 1. The lead was duly picked up and several of those present argued that the problem was not really with the theory of Dirac but rather in the way it was used. Of course, Tomonaga, Schwinger and Feynman eventually confirmed it.

During one of the lectures the speaker wrote something on the board. Someone from the audience then asked: "Is there not a logarithm?" The speaker replied: "When I do it decently, the logarithm will be there." Then Bethe remarked: "When it is done *really* decently, there is no logarithm." (Laughter).

About the conference, the leading newspaper *The New York Herald Tribune* had this to say:

> Twenty three of the country's best known theoretical physicists—the men who made the atomic bomb—gathered together in a rural inn to begin three days of discussion and study, during which they hope to straighten out a few of the difficulties that beset modern physics.
>
> It is doubtful if there has ever been a conference quite like this one. The physicists, backed by the National Academy of Science, have taken over Ram's Head Inn … They roam through the corridors mumbling mathematical equations, eat their meals amid the fury of technical discussions and gather regularly in the lobby for blackboard discussion …
>
> … The conference is taking place with almost complete informality, aided by the fact that the scientists have the inn all to themselves and feel that there is no one to mind if they take off their coats and get to work …

After the conference Oppenheimer thanked Jewett and wrote:

> The three days were a joy to us, and perhaps rather unexpectedly fruitful; we had a long needed chance for clarification and exchange of views and came away a good deal more certain of the directions in which progress may lie.

I cannot help slipping in here an Oppenheimer story. After the Shelter Island Conference, Oppenheimer was to fly to Boston to receive an honorary degree from the Harvard University. However, bad weather forced his plane to come down at the New London Coast Guard Station which was not open to civilian aircraft. The pilot was Worried because he was not supposed to land there. Sure enough the party was met by a menacing naval officer, ready to arrest them all. Oppenheimer whispered to the pilot, "Don't worry." He then stretched out his arm and told the navy man, "Officer, my name is Oppenheimer." The bewildered officer asked, "The Oppenheimer?" to which Oppenheimer replied, "An Oppenheimer." Once the big man was recognised, the red carpet was promptly unrolled! The party was duly wined and dined and later Oppenheimer was taken with military escort to the station and put on the train to Boston.

Getting back to the conference itself, the highlight was the report by Lamb on his results. The audience was electrified and suggestions poured in about how the Lamb shift could be calculated. On the train back to Cornell, Bethe actually worked it all out (though in a non-relativistic manner) and found that the measured value for the Lamb shift could be substantially accounted for. As one historian later recalled:

> This had not at all been obvious at Shelter Island. Bethe's calculation was crucial and confirmed the feeling expressed at Shelter Island that the effect was a quantum electrodynamical one.

Here is Bethe's own recollection:

> It [the Lamb shift] was a wonderful new effect—completely unexpected! It tied in with the old puzzle of the infinite self-energy … To calculate the shift in the spectral lines, one should only consider the difference between the self-energy of a free electron, and the self-energy of an electron in a field, like the electron in the hydrogen atom. A relativistic calculation was far beyond my ability to do in any short time. I knew that the self-energy diverges in the logarithmic case. That had been known since 1934. So I said, all right, I'll get the non-relativistic part [of the Lamb shift]. I finished the calculation in the course of the train ride.

Curiously, till he received a copy of Bethe's paper, Lamb himself thought that the effect observed by him was not of electromagnetic origin.

On 9th June (less than a week after the conference), Bethe sent a copy of his paper to Oppenheimer, adding:

> You see it does work. Also, the second term already gives a finite result and is not zero as we thought during the conference. In fact, its logarithmic divergence makes the order of magnitude correct. It also seems that Vicky [Weisskopf] and Schwinger are correct that the hole theory is probably important in order to obtain convergence.

6.3 The Feynman story

We now come to the trio mentioned at the beginning of Chapter 1, and the role they played. We start with Feynman, certainly the most colourful of the three. The Feynman story begins around 1937 when he was a student in the prestigious Massachussetts Institute of Technology. Recalling those days Feynman says:

> I was an undergraduate student reading about the known physics, learning slowly about all these things that people were worrying about, and realising that ultimately the fundamental problem of the day was that the quantum theory of electricity and magnetism was not completely satisfactory. This I gathered from books like those of Heitler and Dirac. I was inspired by the remarks in these books; not by the parts in which everything was proved and demonstrated carefully, because I couldn't understand those very well … The last sentence of the book of Dirac I still remember, "It seems that some essentially new physical ideas are needed." So, I had this as a challenge and an inspiration.

Feynman decided not to bother about what had already been done and to concentrate instead on the challenge ahead. The unwanted infinities were clearly the target and he had some ideas about how to tackle them. He says:

> It seemed to me quite evident that the idea a particle acts on itself, that the electrical force acts on the same particle that generates it, is not a necessary one—it is sort of silly, as a matter of fact. And so I suggested to myself that electrons cannot act on themselves, they can act only on other electrons. That means there is no field at all.

Don't get shocked! That is the way Feynman is. He is here trying to kill two birds with one stone. By saying an electron cannot interact with itself, he is getting rid of the self-energy problem. By abolishing the field, he is wiping out the infinite degrees of freedom associated with the (virtual) photon field which he believes is the source of infinities. He is not at all perturbed that he might appear like Don Quixote fighting wi dmills! He says:

> The law of force connecting the motion of one charge with another would involve a delay. Shake this one, that one shakes later … I don't let the electron act on itself … hence, no self-energy! … You

> see then my general plan was to first solve the classical problem, to get rid of the infinite self-energies in the classical theory, and to hope that when I made a quantum theory of it, everything would be just fine.
>
> That was the beginning, and the idea seemed so obvious to me and so elegant that I fell deeply in love with it. And, like falling in love with a woman, it is only possible if you do not know much about her so you cannot see her faults.

Feynman now moved over to Princeton to do a Ph.D. under the guidance of Wheeler. He continued to think about electrodynamics, and somewhere along the line began to learn what was wrong with the idea that an electron cannot act on itself. If the self-force was abolished, then F_{rad} (see equation 4.12) would also disappear along with it and this, one could not afford since radiation resistance was a fact of life. Then followed a period of lively dialogue with Wheeler and together they discovered that F_{rad} too could be described in terms of other electrons, as pointed out in Chapter 4. Feynman recalls:

> Many months were devoted to checking all these points. I worked to show that everything is independent of the shape of the container and so on, that the laws are exactly right … and that there was in fact no logical difficulty with the theory. It was perfectly satisfactory.
>
> We also found that we could reformulate this thing in another way, and that is by the principle of least action … So all of classical electrodynamics was contained in this very simple form. It looked good, and therefore, it was undoubtedly true, at least to the beginner.

So this was one solution to the classical electrodynamics in which the electric field played no role at all! One could of course reinstate the field in a particular way; one could modify electrical interactions themselves by the $\delta \to f$ replacement. In general, several possible solutions to the problems of classical electrodynamics were being explored; the hope was that at least one of them would provide a good starting point to deal with the difficulties of QED II. Along the line, Feynman was slowly beginning to "develop a healthy disrespect for the Hamiltonian method of describing physics." Why? Because in that method the future evolves from the past and

> you need a lot of book keeping variables to keep track of what the particles did in the past; These are called field variables. You will, also, have to tell what the field is at the present moment, if you are

able to see later what is going to happen. From the overall space time point of view of the least action principle, the field appears as nothing but book keeping variables insisted on by the Hamiltonian method.

Once again a dislike for fields, and you see why Feynman was moving away from the traditional Hamiltonian method. He wanted to do electrodynamics without being bothered with a lot of book keeping, i.e., keeping track of the (virtual) field variables.

One day, Feynman received a phone call from Wheeler in which the latter said (—this is Feynman again, recalling):

"Feynman, I know why all the electrons have the same charge and the same mass." "Why?" "Because, they are all the same electron!"

Wheeler's idea is really wild. He is proposing that there is only one electron in the Universe which zig-zags in space-time! See Fig. 6.1.

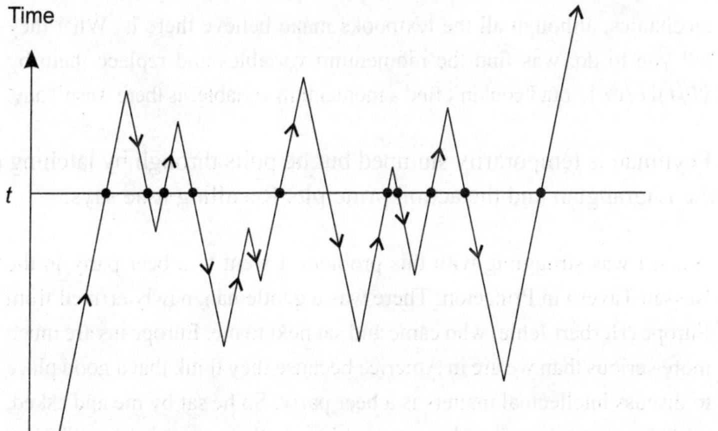

Fig.6.1 Schematic of Wheeler's point of view. According to this, there is only one electron in the whole Universe. Sketched above is its world line. Suppose an observer takes a peep into the Universe at time t. To him it would appear there are many electrons and positrons in the Universe because the scenario he sees would be determined by the intersection of the horizontal line above with the world line of the electron. Feynman did not agree with this picture but conceded that it was a good idea to think of the electron going back in time and mimicking the positron.

We poor humans take a cut of space-time at some instant of time and this cut intersects the world line of this (one and only) electron at many places whereupon we immediately jump to the conclusion that there are many electrons! Feynman doesn't agree. They have an argument (on the phone). What about an electron back tracking in time? That, says Wheeler, is a positron. But then, says Feynman, there aren't as many positrons in this Universe as electrons. The two disagree. However, Feynman took one idea of Wheeler very seriously, namely "that positrons could simply be represented as electrons going from the future to the past in a back section of their world lines. That, I stole!"

With this new idea in hand Feynman was now convinced that he had solved the conceptual problems facing him in classical physics, and all that remained was to carry it all over to the quantum world. About this he says:

> Now there is no unique way to make a quantum theory from classical mechanics, although all the textbooks make believe there is. What they tell you to do, was find the momentum variables and replace them by $(\hbar/i)(\partial/\partial x)$, but I couldn't find a momentum variable, as there wasn't any.

Feynman is temporarily stumped but he pulls through by latching on to the Lagrangian and the action principle. Recalling it he says:

> When I was struggling with this problem, I went to a beer party in the Nassau Tavern in Princeton. There was a gentleman, newly arrived from Europe (Herbert Jehle) who came and sat next to me. Europeans are much more serious than we are in America because they think that a good place to discuss intellectual matters is a beer party. So he sat by me and asked, "What are you doing" and so on, and I said, "I am drinking beer." Then I realised that he wanted to know what work I was doing and I told him I was struggling with this problem, and I simply turned to him and said, "Listen, do you know any way of doing quantum mechanics, starting with action—where the action integral comes from quantum mechanics?" "No," he said, "but Dirac has a paper in which the Lagrangian, at least, comes into quantum mechanics. I will show it to you tomorrow."
>
> Next day we went to the Princeton Library … and he showed me this paper. What Dirac said was the following: There is in quantum mechanics a very important quantity which carries the wave function from one time to another, besides the differential equation but

> equivalent to it, a kind of kernel, which we might call $K(x', x)$, which carries the wave function $\psi(x)$ at time t to the wave function $\psi(x')$ at time $t + \varepsilon$.

Feynman got the clue he was looking for and a few days later lying in bed he had the whole thing figured out, at least conceptually. All this was useful in getting the doctorate degree! Meanwhile the war intervened and Feynman went to Los Alamos to work on the atom bomb project. He says:

> During the war I did not have time to work on these things very extensively, but wandered about on buses and so forth, with little pieces of paper and struggled to work…

After the war, Feynman joined Cornell University as a staff member. Bethe was a Professor there. I have already told you about the Shelter Island conference and Bethe's paper written on the train during the return journey. Let us now hear from Feynman.

> Returning to Cornell, he [Bethe] gave a lecture on the subject which I attended. He explained that it gets very confusing to figure out which infinite term corresponds to what in trying to make the correction for the infinite change in mass. If there were any modifications whatsoever at high frequencies (even though not physically correct), then there would be no problem at all to figuring out how to keep track of everything. You just calculate, the finite mass correction Δm to the electron mass m_0, substitute the numerical values of $m_0 + \Delta m$ for m_0 in the results for any other problem and all these ambiguities would be resolved. If, in addition, the method were relativistically invariant, then we would be absolutely sure …
>
> After the lecture, I went up to him and told him, "I can do that [relativistic calculation] for you, I'll bring it in for you tomorrow." I guess I knew every way to modify quantum electrodynamics known to man at the time.

So the next day, Feynman and Bethe get together. Feynman explains his bag of tricks—action principle, path integral, $\delta \rightarrow f$ conversion and all that—and together they try to see if the self-energy comes out finite. Till this point, Feynman had never used his fancy ideas for dealing with any real and practical problem. This was, so to speak, the first time his method was being tried out. And instead of obtaining a finite answer, Bethe and Feynman obtained a divergence like v^6—this was much worse than the logarithmic divergence of Weisskopf.

Feynman went home disappointed. He was convinced that some mistake had been committed during the calculations, and that his method was perfectly OK. He also realised that he had neglected practical problems and practical tools.

> I remember that when someone tried to teach me about annihilation and creation operators, that this, operator creates an electron, I said, "How do you create an electron? It disagrees with the conservation of charge," and in that way, I blocked my mind from learning a very practical scheme of calculation.

Some process of self learning was needed which Feynman then went through. This paid off. One day at a meeting of the American Physical Society, a person named Slotnick presented a calculation of the neutron – electron interaction. Slotnick got two answers and they were not the same; everyone wondered why. Feynman went home thinking and had it all figured out by the next morning. Let us now hear Feynman himself.

> The next day at the meeting I saw Slotnick and said, "Slotnick, I worked it out last night; I wanted to see if I got the same answers you do …" And he said, "What do you mean you worked it out last night; it took me six months!"

Anyway, they had a huddle and Feynman was able to make his argument. But it was more important than just scoring a point over Slotnick. Feynman says:

> That was a thrilling moment for me like receiving the Nobel Prize, because that convinced me, at last, I did have some kind of a method and technique and understood how to do something that other people did not know how to do.

What Feynman is trying to say is that he had a manifestly covariant way of doing quantum mechanics and could apply it to electrodynamics. It is interesting that unlike Schwinger or for that matter Tomonaga, Feynman was not too concerned about making numerical calculations of radiative corrections using his method. As someone remarked, he was after bigger fish. But Feynman sought it in his own style. Not for him deriving everything systematically starting with a clean sheet of paper and a few basic assumptions. As he himself said,

> I did know from experience, from fooling around, that everything was, in fact, equivalent to the regular electrodynamics and had partial proofs of many pieces, although I never really sat down, like Euclid did for the geometers of Greece, and made sure that you could get it all from a single simple set of axioms [which was Schwinger's style too]. As a result the work was criticized …

Of course, this criticism was only in the very early days when people didn't quite understand what he was trying to do, which is reasonable since at that time few knew about this third way of doing QM. Fortunately, Feynman stayed with retarded waves alone, although he permitted the $\delta \rightarrow f$ equation here change. He kept away from the view of the public the "half-advanced and half-retarded" theory he and Wheeler had invented together (for classical electrodynamics). Had he done so, there would have been even greater disbelief.

One last remark about Feynman's contribution and that is about the diagrams. Years later he said:

> I don't know when I started to make such pictures. I do remember at one particular stage … noticing how *funny* they looked. I was sort of half-dreaming, like a kid would, that it might some day be interesting, that it would be funny if these funny pictures turned out to be useful, because *the damn Physical Review* would be *full* of these odd-looking things. And that turned out to be true.

6.4 On the other side of the Pacific

On now to the Tomonaga part of the story, and we start in 1932 when Tomonaga joined Nishina in Tokyo. His early work (with Nishina) was on the neutron and the problem of nuclear forces. It was around that time that Dirac published his paper introducing a relativistic formulation of quantum mechanics, especially the mechanics of electrons interacting with an electromagnetic field. About this paper Tomonaga says:

> This paper of Dirac attracted my interest because of the novelty of its philosophy and the beauty of its form.Nishina also showed a great interest in this paper and suggested that I investigate the possibility of predicting some new phenomena by this theory. Then I started computations to see whether the Klein-Nishina formula could be derived from this theory …

Earlier, Pauli and Heisenberg had published their own version of relativistic quantum mechanics. During a brief visit to the Soviet Union (now defunct!), Dirac along with Fock and Podolsky (whose name would appear again in Part III) showed that the work of Pauli and Heisenberg was in fact equivalent to his own. There were problems with both theories—it is intesting that Pauli and Heisenberg on the one hand and Dirac on the other expressed critical opinions of each other's work!—but Tomonaga was attracted to the Dirac version as it seemed to offer some interesting possibilities. However, they became evident only somewhat later.

In 1937 Tomonaga went to Germany to work in Heisenberg's institute in Leipzig. I should mention that much earlier in 1932, Tomonaga had heard both Dirac and Heisenberg lecture on quantum mechanics in Tokyo. Tomonaga stayed two years in Germany working mainly on problems in nuclear physics. In those days there was not the specialisation that one sees now and people comfortably moved from problems in atomic physics to problems in nuclear physics. Later Tomonaga would submit part of his researches as his thesis to the Tokyo University for getting his doctorate degree.

Tomonaga does not seem to have been happy in Germany. In his diary he writes:

> It has been cold and drizzling since morning and I have devoted the whole day to physics in vain. As it got dark I went to the park. The sky was grey with a bit of yellow, of twilight in it. I could see the silhouetted white birch grove glowing vaguely in the dark. My view was partly obscured by my tired eyes; my nose prickled from cold and upon returning home I had a nosebleed. After supper I took up my physics again, but at last I gave up. Ill-starred work indeed!
>
> Recently I have felt very sad without any reason; so I went to see a film … Returning home I read a book on physics. I don't understand it very well. Meanwhile I suffer … Why isn't Nature clearer and more directly comprehensible?

Suddenly, physics was beginning to lose its charm and as he put it, "I was no longer interested in the existence of the neutron, neutrino…" He continues:

> I complained in emotional words to Professor Nishina about the slump in my work, whereupon I got his letter in reply this morning. After reading it my eyes were filled with tears … He says: only fortune decides your progress in achievements. All of us stand on the

> dividing line from which the future is invisible. We need not be too anxious about the results even though they may turn out to be quite different from what you expect. By and by you may meet a new chance for success …

As I told you, Tomonaga was working on problems in nuclear physics under the supervison of Heisenberg. The latter had just completed a simple classical calculation related to self-energy effects in meson problems and suggested that Tomonaga look at this thing more closely. Tomonaga says:

> Heisenberg, in this paper published in 1939, emphasised that the field reaction would be crucial in meson – nucleon scattering. … I still vividly remember how Heisenberg enthusiastically explained this idea to me and handed me galley proofs of his forthcoming paper. Influenced by Heisenberg, I came to believe that the problem of field reaction from being meaningless was one which required a frontal attack.

Tomonaga wanted to continue his stay in Leipzig and do a quantum version of Heisenberg's classical theory. But war clouds were gathering and so Tomonaga decided to return to Japan. On the way he stopped over for a day in New York to see the World Fair. About returning Tomonaga says, "When I was in Germany I had wanted to stay another year, but once 1 was aboard a Japanese ship I became eager to arrive in Japan."

Back in Japan, Tomonaga tinkered with a few problems in meson physics but also turned his attention to developing a proper relativistic theory of quantum mechanics. A year earlier, Yukawa too had considered the question of developing a relativistically invariant theory as also that of countering the divergences or the infinities. Yukawa was obviously trying to kill two birds with one stone but Tomonaga preferred to tackle one problem at a time. Thus in 1943, he wrote a paper entiltled *Relativistically Invariant Formulation of Quantum Field Theory*. Needless to say that this paper leaned heavily on the earlier work of Dirac already referred to. The paper was written in Japanese, and the world knew about it only in 1946 when an English translation of it appeared in the journal of *Progress in Theoretical Physics* (published in Japan).

By this time (i.e., 1942) Japan had entered the war, and Tomonaga moved over to war-oriented work. Like many of his counterparts in

America, he became involved in theoretical work related to magnetrons and radar. Miyazima, an engineer, recalls:

> One day our boss Dr. Nishina took me to see several engineers at the Naval Technical Research Institute. They had been engaged in the research and development of powerful split-anode magnetrons … Since they were engineers, their way of thinking was characteristic of engineers … but unfortunately it was completely foreign to me … Every time I met them, I used to report to Tomonaga how I could not understand them.

This is a common problem, the lack of proper communication between physicists and engineers because their thinking tends to be different. But Tomonaga promptly solved Miyazima's difficulty by describing the motion of the electrons in the magnetron in physicist's language and explaining how secular perturbation theory such as is used in classical mechanics could be applied.

Likewise, when dealing with the problem of propagation of electromagnetic waves in waveguides, he found that the engineers were using the old language of impedance. Instead he cast everything in terms of matrices, greatly simplifying the problem.

Japan and Germany were fighting the war on the same side (in contrast to the First World War), and exchanges between the two often took place via submarine traffic. You might remember that Netaji Subhas Chandra Bose went to Japan from Germany in a submarine. One such submarine landing in Japan brought a secret document for Tomonaga from Heisenberg. As he tore open the envelope stamped secret all over, Tomonaga wondered what it contained. It was nothing but Heisenberg's paper (later to become famous) on the *S*-matrix. Heisenberg was keen to send his latest reprint and to make it qualify for a submarine ride, he had to mark it secret!

In late 1945, the Pacific war ended (Germany had surrendered in May but the war with Japan went on till August. Japan yielded only after Hiroshima and Nagasaki were blasted with atom bombs). Japan was completely shattered and everyone was engaged in picking up the pieces. Tomonaga went back to physics and started now on the idea of using his new formalism (developed in 1943) to calculating certain quantities which earlier gave infinite answers. Back in 1939, Dancoff in the U.S. had done a relativistic calculation of electron – electron scattering. Tomonaga applied his new methods and found that "what took a few months in the Dancoff type of calculation could now be done in a few weeks." And now the Japanese group discovered that

Dancoff had made an error in his calculations. Tomonaga has declared that if only Dancoff had not made this unfortunate error, the history of renormalisation would have been different; we would never know! To get back to the story, Japanese physicists were now rather cutoff from current developments which were taking place mainly in the U.S. About this, Tomonaga recalls:

> After the Second World War it was quite difficult in Japan to obtain information from abroad. But soon we got the news that in the U.S., Lewis and Epstein found Dancoff's mistake and gave the same conclusion as ours, Schwinger constructed a covariant field theory similar to ours, and he was probably performing various calculations making use of it. In particular, little by little news arrived that the so-called Lamb shift was discovered … and that Bethe was calculating it theoretically. The first information concerning the Lamb shift was obtained not through the *Physical Review*, but through the popular science column of a weekly U.S. magazine [Newsweek]. This information about the Lamb shift prompted us to begin a calculation more exactly than Bethe's tentative one.

Actually, even by 1945, the Japanese physicists had started making calculations of radiative corrections. But cut off as they were, they did not make calculations pertaining to problems of real interest; instead, they were tackling problems like Compton scattering. According to Dyson, "The isolation of these Japanese workers has undoubtedly constituted a serious loss to theoretical physics."

In April 1948, Tomonaga sent Oppenheimer a collection of his papers. Acknowledging it, Oppenheimer sent a telegram: "Grateful for your letter and papers. Found most interesting and valuable mostly paralleling much work done here. Strongly suggest you write a summary account of present state and views for prompt publication *Physical Review*. Glad to arrange." Tomonaga responded by writing up the account that Oppenheimer wanted. The Tomonaga part of our story ends here. There remains the Schwinger part, to which we now turn.

6.5 The Schwingerian touch

Schwinger's career shows four distinct phases: From 1934 to 1946, preparation. 1947, non-relativistic theory. 1947–1948, first relativistic results. 1949–1950, a polished version of a relativistically covariant theory. In 1934 at the early age of 16, Schwinger wrote a paper in which he used Dirac's result to deal with the quantum electrodynamics of electrons interacting with each other. The paper was not published but it is remarkable in that the interaction representation idea was already introduced by him in this work.

After the war, there was a lot of interest in developing new and powerful accelerators. Schwinger joined the effort, and put relativity and electromagnetic theory to practical use. Came then the Shelter Island conference during which the Lamb shift was announced. Schwinger now had his work cut out. But he had to take a couple of months off to get married and go wandering across the country with his wife! Once these matrimonial obligations were discharged, he got started. Schwinger recalls:

> There was this effect [Lamb shift]. It wasn't infinite and it wasn't zero … Here was an experiment saying it's not infinite [as many theories did] and it's not zero [as Dirac's theory did]; it's small, it's finite—we've got to understand it …
>
> Electrodynamics was conceived to be *wrong*. There was a whole generation dedicated to changing it … Very few people—and I count myself first and foremost—said, "Let's go back and look at the original theory." … What I brought to the problem was a physical instinct and an ability to do calculations. That's all that was needed.

The Lamb shift, as Bethe showed, could be accounted for almost entirely without the use of relativity. But there was another effect which could not be explained without relativity. Schwinger tells us about it:

> The magnetic moment of the electron, which came from Dirac's relativistic theory, was something that *no* non-relativistic theory could describe correctly. It was a fundamentally relativistic problem … That's the one I jumped on … I got the wrong answer. I got the wrong answer because in my calculation the magnetic moment that you recognise when the electron is at rest and the magnetic moment that you recognise when it's moving in the atom under the action of its electric field turned out not to be the same. Which meant that the methods I was using violated relativistic in variance … I was driven to invent a new method that was explicitly relativistic so I would get the same numbers no matter when I looked at the electron.

The first paper on the subject was submitted in December 1947, and is very unSchwingerian if one may say so, because the paper does not contain a single formula or equation! In it Schwinger says:

> The simplest example of a radiative correction is that for the energy of an electron in an external magnetic field. The detailed application of the theory shows that the radiative correction to the magnetic interaction energy corresponds to an additional magnetic moment associated with the electron spin, of magnitude 0.001162.

This is the first announcement to the world about radiative corrections to the magnetic moment of the electron. The world is kept guessing about how Schwinger arrived at this result. Towards the end of March 1948, a conference was arranged which was to be a sequel to the Shelter Island meeting. This one was held at a place called the Pocono Manor Inn. Recalling, Schwinger says:

> The Pocono conference was my first opportunity to learn what Feynman was doing with quantum electrodynamics. I had seen his work with John A. Wheeler on classical electrodynamics, and the idea of abolishing the electromagnetic field, in a fundamental sense, did not appeal to me at all.

See also Box 6.1.

Box 6.1 The Shelter Island Conference threw the QED problem wide open. People realised that there was this Lamb shift and it had to be explained. Bethe of course showed the way but that was not enough. One needed a proper theoretical machinery to make calculations without being bothered by divergences, and this is what Feynman and Schwinger had been working on (in America) after the historic Shelter Island Conference. Their chance to present their work came during the follow-up conference held in March 1948 in Pocono Manor, Pennsylvania.

During this conference, Schwinger gave a five hour lecture that overwhelmed all present. Then came Feynman with his diagrams which had many puzzled. Bohr who was present, shook his head and muttered: "We can't draw electron trajectories ... They went out in 1928 with the advent of the Uncertainty principle."

So there it was. People generally knew that these two had done something but were unable to understand what it was. How was it between Feynman and Schwinger? Feynman recalls:

> I talked to Schwinger in the halls. And we had *no difficulty* with each other. We had *faith* in each other. If he would say something,

> I wouldn't argue that his equations might be wrong. If I'd say, "I'd do it this way," he didn't bother. He didn't even try to understand it. And I didn't try to understand his equations. But we could understand each other … because we had done the same problem.

In Tamil there is a proverb which says that even an elephant can slip. Let us now hear about how Schwinger slipped.

> It was when we turned to an electrostatic field, to the relativistic justification and extension of the Bethe calculation, that an unfortunate bit of confusion entered. The problem was the joining of the relativistic calculation, where the Coulomb potential is regarded as perturbation, to the nonrelativistic calculation, which treats the Coulomb potential exactly. Later developments would avoid that un-physical separation, but the first attacks used it. And both Feynman and I goofed-we blew it [the reference here is to the (11/24) term in (3.9)].

The next paper of Schwinger appeared in early 1949. Like his first one on QED, it also was short and dealt with radiative corrections, this time with reference to electron scattering. Unlike earlier, there was a sprinkling of formulae, besides a few numbers of interest to experimentalists. With this, Schwinger enters the last of the four phases identified earlier. As he puts it,

> The impetus of experimental discoveries of 1947 was waning. The pressure to account for those results had produced a certain theoretical structure that was perfectly adequate for the original task, but demanded simplification and generalisation; a new vision was required.

6.6 Taking it to the masses

It is useful to pause and recap events briefly. Tomonaga and Schwinger had worried about a relativistic formulation of quantum theory which would be free from defects the earlier versions had. Independently, Feynman was engaged in creating an entirely new approach to quantum mechanics based on the action principle. Tomonaga had published a few bits and pieces here and there, mostly in Japanese. Both Schwinger and Feynman had plenty of ideas but had hardly published anything.

Then came the Shelter Island meeting and all of a sudden people were calculating the Lamb shift by one method or the other. But barring Schwinger and Feynman (and of course Tomonaga in Japan), no one else had the complete tool kit so to speak. Schwinger announced to the world his possession of the tool kit through a few short communications in which he reported numbers obtained after radiative corrections. Feynman had his own way of doing it all with diagrams, though he hadn't sat down to calculating actual numbers. In short, in 1948, barring a few who had met or heard Feynman or Schwinger, the "masses" at large had no clue about the new technology, except that Schwinger had used it effectively.

At this stage, Freeman Dyson entered the picture and did yeoman service. A few words about this outstanding theoretical physicist. Dyson belongs to the class of physicists who solve problems rather than create new theories. Born in England in 1923, he was educated at the University of Cambridge. During the Second World War, he was at the headquarters of the Royal Air Force (RAF) Bomber command, doing operations research. One of his jobs was to analyse the effectiveness of night bombing of Germany by the RAF. After the war he went to Cornell, and later joined the Institute for Advanced Study in Princeton (of which Oppenheimer was the Director).

In 1948, Dyson published two long tutorial papers which explained clearly the relationship between the apparently different approaches of Feynman on the one hand and Schwinger and Tomonaga on the other. In addition, he showed "how the Schwinger theory can be applied to specific problems in such a way as to incorporate the ideas of Feynman." Further, he linked Feynman's version to the earlier *S*-matrix theory of Heisenberg. In this way he brought out lucidly and clearly the advantages of using Schwinger's approach for bound-state problems, and the virtues of the Feynman approach for scattering problems. It is not that Dyson merely unified the work of Feynman and Tomonaga/Schwinger or even analysed technical issues connected with renormalisation. In 1948/1949, the papers of Dyson were the only detailed papers on the other subject; those of Feynman and Schwinger appeared somewhat later. And as far as Schwinger's papers are concerned, one wonders how many found them useful!

6.7 The end of the trail

We are now into 1949–1950. Back to Schwinger. He was conscious that QED was rapidly becoming an industry. Commenting on it he remarked,

> Like the silicon chip of more recent years, the Feynman diagram was bringing computation to the masses. Yes, one can analyse experience into individual pieces of topology. But eventually one has to put it all together again. And then the piecemeal approach loses some of its attraction.

Schwinger now went into a retreat later to come out and dazzle the world with a series of papers nicknamed the New Opus. They are typically Schwingerian, and the masses can only admire them from afar! No wonder the remark has been made that while others write papers to show it can be done Schwinger writes papers to show that only he can do it!

Our story is about to end. Let us go back to Feynman and his "love affair" and how he viewed it looking back. He says:

> So what happened to the old theory I fell in love with as a youth? Well, I would say it's become an old lady, that has very little attraction left in her and the young today will not have their hearts pound when they look at her anymore. But, we can say the best we can for any old woman, that she has been a very good mother and she has given birth to some very good children …

We shall briefly meet these offsprings in the next chapter.

7 Beyond QED

In this volume we have been primarily concerned with QED. It is actually a branch of a general subject called *quantum field theory* and historically, was the first to make its appearance. We have seen how the fortunes of QED have fluctuated. Thanks to renormalisation etc., QED (version III) is today what Weisskopf calls "a spotless example of a physical theory."

QED, versions I, II and even III, emerged as extensions of the original attempt to develop a logical and consistent quantum theory. But obviously, QED is not designed to explain the whole of Nature. For example, according to the QED picture, the neutron which is an electrically neutral particle, has no business having a magnetic moment; and yet it has. Clearly therefore, any attempt to comprehensively explain Nature must make room not only for the other forces (besides the electromagnetic), but also for various internal degrees of freedom (e.g. colour), associated with the denizens of the elementary particle world. This is an exercise that has been going for many years. Some progress has been made but no one will claim that the end is in sight.

QED features the interaction between electrons and photons. Electrons are Fermions and photons are Bosons. The latter are the quanta of the force field. All elementary particles known to date are either Fermions or Bosons. No wonder physicists have resorted to QED-like methods in dealing with them.

The first example of such an attempt goes back to the mid-thirties when Hideki Yukawa in Japan sought to describe the nuclear forces between protons and neutrons (both of which are Fermions) as due to the exchange of a Boson which now is called the π-meson. Passing references to this were made in the last chapter while describing Tomonaga's contributions. No mediating particle like the π-meson was known at that time and so Yukawa's conjecture was a bold one indeed. The predicted meson was discovered roughly ten years later, and Yukawa was duly rewarded with the Nobel Prize. Actually, nuclear forces have turned out to be a lot more complicated than Yukawa had imagined but that does not detract from the beauty of his prediction.

Starting from the thirties, extensive studies have been made of radioactivity and the forces responsible for it namely, *weak interaction*. It was then discovered that electromagnetic interactions and weak interaction are really, so to speak, two sides of the same coin. At first sight this is most surprising since the electromagnetic interaction is long-ranged (it can act literally over the entire Universe) whereas the range of the weak interaction is less than 10^{-12}cm. No two forces could be so dissimilar and yet Nature has ordained a link between the two. Once this link became evident, it was natural to extend the original QED to encompass weak interactions. The result is *Quantum electro-weak dynamics* (QEWD). If Feynman, Schwinger and Tomonaga were the heroes in the development of QED (version III), the stars associated with the new development were Salam, Weinberg and Glashow. Like the earlier trio, they too shared the Nobel Prize.

The appetite grows by what it feeds on. Same here. Taking a cue from Yukawa and drawing upon all the recent experience? vigorous efforts have been made to develop a field theory for strong interactions (which mediate nuclear forces). In the thirties, it was believed that the neutron and the proton were the basic building blocks of the nuclear world but current thinking is that it is quarks which do this job.

The family of quarks is sizeable and in addition they have all kinds of unusual properties. This is not the place to dwell on all that but I must point out certain basic analogies which are given below.

Electrodynamics	*Strong interactions*
electron	quarks
(electric) charge	"colour"
photon	gluons

The field theory for strong interactions based- on the above analogies is called *quantum chromodynamics* (QCD). In QED it is charge which is the source of the field. Analogously, in QCD it is the property whimsically called *colour* which is the source of the field (see also Box 7.1).

Box 7.1 In the twelfth Solvay Congress (in 1961), Feynman and Dirac met for the first time. The following is their conversation, as reported by Pais:

F: I am Feynman.

D: I am Dirac. (Silence.)

F: It must be wonderful to be the discoverer of that equation.

D: What are you working on?

F: Mesons.

D: Are you trying to discover an equation for them?

F: It is very hard.

D: One must try.

This was long before QCD, and in those days some even believed that field theory did not apply to strong interactions.

QCD is an active field and a rather complicated one too. I cannot go into it here but two aspects of it must be mentioned. In both QED and QCD there are basically two players; in one case it is the electron and the photon while in the other it is the quark and the gluon. All Feynman diagrams in QED are essentially built up from the basic diagram in Fig. 7.1(a). By contrast, in QCD there are three basic diagrams as in Fig. 7.1(b). The second difference between the two field theories concerns the behaviour of the coupling constant. I have already introduced you to the coupling constant of QED. There is a similar constant in the case of QCD and the behaviour of the two as a function of distance is compared in Fig. 7.2. The large value of the coupling constant at large values of r poses serious problems in applying perturbation theory. This is typical of the rough terrain associated with QCD. But all that has not deterred brave souls from venturing out there. No doubt at present there are many dark clouds hanging but one expects that there would be a breakthrough, bringing out the Sun.

From the foregoing, it should be. clear that various field theories one has today are imitations of each other. You might wonder: "Why are all the theories of physics so similar in their structure?" Feynman has a comment:

> There are a number of possibilities. The first is the limited imagination of physicists: When we see a new phenomenon we try to fit it into the framework we already have—until we have made enough

experiments. So when some fool physicist gives a lecture at UCLA [University of California, Los Angeles] and says, "This is the way it works, and look how wonderfully similar the theories are," it is not because Nature is *really* similar; it is because the physicists have been able to think of the same damn thing over and over again.

Another possibility is that it *is* the same damn thing over and over again—that Nature has only one way of doing things, and She repeats her story from time to time.

The latter appears to be the majority view at present, and hence the popularity of field theories.

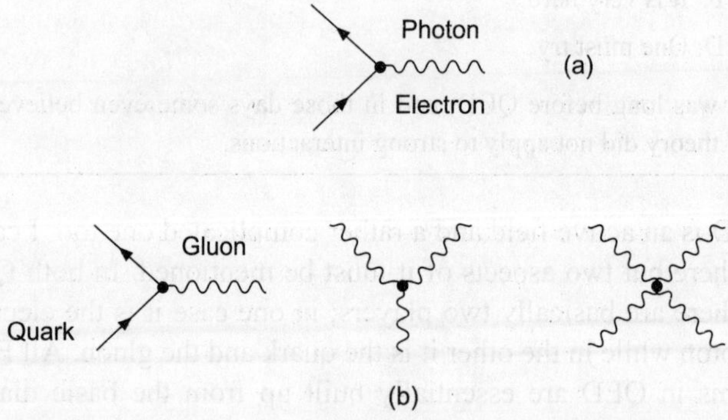

Fig.7.1 (a) Basic module or diagram element of QED. By contrast, there are three basic bricks or building blocks in QCD as in (b).

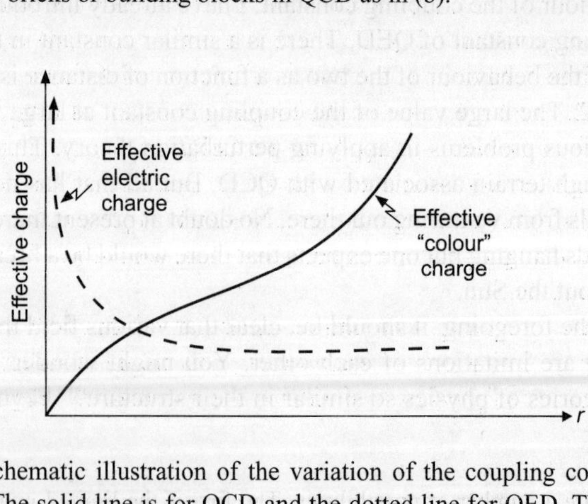

Fig.7.2 Schematic illustration of the variation of the coupling constant with distance. The solid line is for QCD and the dotted line for QED. The large increase in Q_{eff} in the latter case as $r \to \infty$ implies that a single quark cannot exist as a free particle.

To put it all in a nutshell, the picture of the world we have today is roughly the following (from a field theorist's point of view, as once paraphased by Dyson): There are about a dozen or so different quantum fields. Each field fills the whole of space and has its own peculiar properties. The Universe consists of nothing else except these fields, between which there are various kinds of interactions. Associated with each field is a type of elementary particle. Particles of a given type are identical and indistinguishable. The number of particles of a given type is not fixed, and particles are constantly being created or annihilated and so on.

It is really a melting pot but a creative adventure for those bristling with ideas. But ideas alone are not enough because the subject is very technical and one must be quite adept with sophisticated mathematical techniques and tools.

I cannot think of a better way of ending this chapter and the book itself than by quoting Dyson who says:

> Even to a hardened theoretical physicist it remains perpetually astonishing that our solid world of trees and stones can be built of quantum fields and nothing else. The quantum field seems far too fluid and insubstantial to be the basic stuff of the universe. Yet we have learned gradually to accept the fact that the laws of quantum mechanics impose their own peculiar rigidity which is alien to our intuitive conceptions but which nonetheless effectively holds the earth in place. We have learned to apply both to ourselves and to our subject, the words of Robert Bridges:
>
> *Our stability is but balance, and*
> *our wisdom lies*
> *In masterful administration of the*
> *unforeseen*

Appendix to Chapter 7

Renormalisation and "subtraction physics" are difficult topics. I wrestled with these concepts for years, and I wouldn't be surprised if you have come to the end of this book without grasping their essence! Perhaps I could make one more attempt at explanation.

1. Classical physics gives simple rules for calculating the force produced on an electron by an applied electric or magnetic field. This force is called the Lorentz force, and the standard formula for the Lorentz force is routinely used for designing TV picture tubes etc.
2. Trouble starts when one tries to do an *ab initio* or first-principles calculation, i.e., when one allows for the force an electron exerts on itself while moving (back reaction). So the total force on the electron is the back reaction plus the applied force, if any.
3. While making calculations using the standard Lorentz force formula (as in para 1 above), we take the electron to have the observed mass m_{exp}. But in a first-principles calculation as in 2, we must use the "bare" mass.
4. The "bare" mass is the mass the electron would have, minus the effects due to back reaction. The latter contributes a mass which we may call the electromagnetic mass.
5. Suppose we try to estimate the "bare" mass by saying:

   Bare mass = Observed mass – e.m. mass.

   We are in trouble because e.m. mass for a point electron is infinity! Which makes the "bare" mass also infinite.
6. We can't have a theory which starts with an infinite mass for the "bare" electron.
7. In quantum theory, the difficulty with infinity gets worse. This was what was found when people first enthusiastically applied Dirae's theory to electro dynamical problems.
8. From about 1932 to 1948 there was a desperate struggle with infinities till Schwinger, Tomonaga and Feynman showed the way (independently).
9. Their recipe had three parts:
   (i) Swear by relativistic in variance at each and every step, i.e., make the theory relativistically covariant.
   (ii) Watch out for the trouble makers—self-energy effects, vertex

effects and vacuum polarisation effects. All three can raise their ugly heads, though to different extents in different problems. Each of them must be carefully handled.

(iii) Instead of working with m_0, work with $(m_0 + \Delta m)$. The infinity that is implicit is then killed by a suitable "counter" term.

10. The result is a theory which is a first-principles theory since it explicitly includes back reaction.
11. As in the case of mass, the bare charge of the electron also gets affected by radiative effects. Thus, two parameters namely the mass and the charge of the electron have to be renormalised in QED.
12. Infinities can arise in every order of perturbation calculations done in QED. However, cancellation is possible in every case. Once the cancellation is done, QED becomes tame and harmless like the usual perturbation theory in which the contributions from the higher orders progressively decrease. In fact, QED becomes astonishingly accurate, fully deserving the title: Jewel of Physics.

Well, I hope this clears any residual doubts!

Suggestions for further reading

QED is a highly technical and specialised topic and there aren't too many elementary books I know of which you can pick up rightaway and read. There is of course the following book by Feynman which you MUST read:

1. Feynman, R.P. QED: *The Strange Theory of Light* and *Matter*, Princeton University Press: Princeton, 1985.

On the historical side, the following volumes offer interesting material:

2. Crease, R.P. and Mann, C.C. *The Second Creation*, Affiliated East-West Press: New Delhi , 1989.

3. Brown, L.M. and Hoddeson, L. (Editors) *The Birth of Particle Physics*, Cambridge University Press: Cambridge, 1983.

See also,

4. Feynman, R.P. Article entitled "Pocono Conference" in *Physics Today*, June 1948.

Index

Note: Page numbers in brackets refer to illustrations